# THE HOUSE
## THAT WOULDN'T
# FALL DOWN

BLACK COUNTRY FAMILY REMINISCENCES

Andrew Edwards

Grosvenor House
Publishing Limited

This book is published by
Grosvenor House Publishing Ltd
Link House
140 The Broadway, Tolworth, Surrey, KT6 7HT.
www.grosvenorhousepublishing.co.uk

A CIP record for this book
is available from the British Library

ISBN 978-1-80381-235-9

# Contents

# Foreword

Ido hope the book I have enjoyed writing, helps to paint a picture of my own Black Country family, its microscopic part in the history of the wonderful area and its beautiful people, many of whom I got to know during decades of work and play and who became lifelong friends.

Amblecote and my parents made me what I am and for that I am eternally grateful. There is a stark beauty in a lot of the Black Country, not so easy to spot by some outside visitors to the county, and I believe most people from this area of our wonderful country have ideals, and a grit and a passion for life that somehow steels you to try to do good, be better, work hard, play hard; with a certain satirical dry Midlands sense of humour and to instil purpose in one's own life.

My wonderful parents gave my brother and I a great start in life through thick and thin, with their own life-changing adversities to deal with, as well as striving to give us the best, or the best they could, not attempting to create us in their own image, just wanting us to think for ourselves as new human beings, without pressuring or bullying, cajoling us and wanting us at least to listen, think for ourselves and then make up our own minds.

I don't know how they kept so calm in attaining what they did for us children.

We didn't turn out too bad, Mum and Dad, Mary and Stan. We love you and always will. For everything you gave us. They asked nothing in return from us but a regular phone call, (an admonishment if we didn't!) a letter, a photo or two, keeping in touch, when our lives took us away from the Black Country, as some people must, to make our careers and our own lives, and, yes, our own mistakes. They let the earth's wind take us where we had to go and I know it wasn't easy for them, but they did it. It was difficult, but they somehow did it.

This book and its lovely family photographs are for you.

# Introduction

I self-published my first book on my own life as a journalist, when I was 75.

I had touched on my early life in Amblecote, near Stourbridge, in the Black Country and decided I wanted to write about my family's long association with the area; in my opinion, a unique part of the country, now part of the ubiquitous West Midlands.

So, this is my second book; a very different book from that detailing my journalistic career, which took me all over the world, reporting on international motorcycle sport, mainly speedway.

This book is Black Country-based, but does wander merrily around the world and back again, with memories of my own, growing up in Amblecote, from 1945, when I was born, to when I left in 1973 for my new job, a golden era of change and stability for the area.

I explore my own parents, Mary and Stan Edwards' lives in the Black Country and their tales when they were growing up. Plus, my brother Dave's recollections, born seven years before me in 1938.

There are stories from my grandfather, Billy Hicks, from his days as glassmaker in Thomas Webb's factory in Amblecote and his involvement in local sport, including football and the Stourbridge "Glassboys", plus his own career as a successful bowls exponent.

Included are memories of my father, Stan, a great sportsman and avid member of the Stourbridge Harriers Athletic Club, later the Stourbridge and Dudley Harriers. He was also an avid park tennis player, along with my mum, and like many of his generation a long-distance bike rider, also along with my mum, as he did not pass his driving test until he was 50!

The couple travelled together in the Black Country, and much further, finding out the area's beauty spots like their beloved Clent Hills and Kinver Edge, taking me along when I was a toddler, giving me an insight into those lovely natural places which have never left me. I still return now and again to reminisce.

They gave me, and my brother, David, our love of nature and for me, my love of sport, my own badminton-playing for over a decade in the Black Country and including my own lifelong love affair with the Cradley Heath speedway club at their Dudley Wood Stadium. All sadly no more, all gone, demolished. As a spectator and later reporter of the sport, I was never, never brave enough to race on a track.

In his older age, my father, before the internet, and before the assistance of desktop publishing, researched a display which was put on public display at Stourbridge

Library; his history of the Stourbridge Harriers Athletic club, with handwritten captions for his photos which he had gathered together for the story. It was a big task, and I was very pleased it was seen by the public and was a deserved success in the town.

Then there's my mum, Mary. She lost her mum when she was 14 years of age and had to care for her dad, Billy, all her married life, living in the same house, with her "hubby", and two children. Five people in a two-bedroomed house. Not easy.

It is all part of this book, family life, in an area of rich industrial heritage, most of which has been lost in the passage of time. I had a head start in writing this book because my mum wrote her own book "many moons ago", as she would say, but actually in the mid-1970s, about her life, her family, her upbringing and it tells of how life in the Black Country was so much harder then, and the values which aren't necessarily as they are now.

The book, which she typed out (having learnt to type with two fingers) on a portable typewriter of some vintage, and not knowing of carbon paper to make a copy, typed it out at least six times to my knowledge so that all the family had one. She did this because she wanted to get it published, but never succeeded.

She wrote in April 1975: "Epilogue, gosh that sounds final. It is said there is a book in all of our lives, and it is perfectly true. This is mine; but having tried three times to get this epistle published, I hold my horses and abide. There was a comment from one firm, 'genuine, but lacks selling value'. So, I am another thwarted writer. Just another effort 'Mary E' has had a bash at, that bears no fruit. A pity to waste it, as it has given me joy writing it."

I decided that her tremendous efforts will not go to waste and have included many passages in this book, which are, with the exception of a couple of paragraphs in my first book, *MCN Days Speedway Nights*, newly published, nearly fifty years after she wrote her own book titled, *One Speck of Ordinary Black Country Ash*.

But what is the Black Country? Where are its boundaries, and were we, living in Amblecote, part of the area? Questions brought about by a comment from my brother, Dave, when I began writing this book. Were we really a Black Country family? Was Mum, as she always told us, Black Country?

Well, I admit, we were "middle class", I suppose. I say suppose because what exactly does middle class mean?

We were not poor, but never had much money to spare. My father, always in regular work, was office staff for most of his life, with skills as an estimator in a steel works. As I say, regular work, but not that well paid, although we owned our own house, courtesy of Grandad. Most of the time, there was but one wage coming into the house as Mum, like most, looked after the children, the house, the meals, and her aged dad at home too, making do and mending much of the time.

Mum had worked in her earlier life, before two of us children came along, in the book binding department of

Mark and Moody Ltd., High Street, Stourbridge, itself a local institution. The shop can trace its ancestry from the 19th century. In my day, in the 60s, I remember its three exquisite arches looking out onto the High Street, either side were windows and the middle arch, the door. Newspapers, records, books, magazines, educational toys, cards; I thought it marvellous. All my early LP records were bought there, where you could ask for them to be played in an open sided booth, before purchase. Only going on a trip to "Brummagem" could you find better.

But Mum, as well as looking after all of us, she it was, I reckon, who planned our holidays in UK resorts so dear to her heart. She used to say, if we can't afford first class (for our holidays) then we will go second, third or fourth class, but we will go. And go we did, twice a year, one week each most years, often in caravans or similar.

Never once did we stay in a hotel, swanky, or otherwise, it was pure self-catering, no car either for many years, until Dad got his first car at 50. It was coaches and trains when we did travel.

Mum was born in Wollaston, maybe not the real Black Country, but a spit to the Fish at Amblecote, which most definitely was, because of its glassmaking industry, and that was always known as a Black Country industry and where her father worked and sweated for nigh on 50 years, in the furnace heat and sulphur and lead -infused fumes as a daily bonus.

Brother Dave says Mum was not really Black Country, but she definitely thought she was, living in a two-up two-down terrace house, with tramlines passing the front door morning and night with the yard for washing and the toilet facilities further on up the garden.

A small amount of looking up free history finds Samuel Griffiths' writing in his 1876 *Griffiths Guide to the Iron Trade of Great Britain*. "The Black Country commences at Wolverhampton, extends a distance of sixteen miles to Stourbridge, eight miles to West Bromwich, penetrating the northern districts through Willenhall to Bentley, The Birchills, Walsall and Darlaston, Wednesbury, Smethwick and Dudley Port, West Bromwich and Hill Top, Brockmoor, Wordsley and Stourbridge. As the atmosphere becomes purer, we get to the higher ground of Brierley Hill, nevertheless here also, as far as the ye can reach, on all sides, tall chimneys vomit forth great clouds of smoke"

He said Wolverhampton was considered the capital of the Black Country.

The area is bounded now by four metropolitan boroughs of Dudley (which includes Stourbridge and Amblecote), Sandwell, Walsall and Wolverhampton.

But here is the nub of the question of where does the Black Country begin and end. No one knows the answer and it is said that no two Black Country men or women will agree where it starts and where it ends! There is no fine line which has been meticulously drawn on any maps, ancient or modern.

I contend I was brought up in the Black Country, although not in poverty, which with respect is not a prerequisite. It helped mould me into what I am, I believe, in the first 28 years of my life and in all of my years in which I returned, I still felt I was returning to my Black Country roots. So, there is no line where the Black Country begins and ends, but maybe it's a feeling, which you get from within and maybe taught at your mother's knee, quite literally in my case.

We "dae spake" (didn't speak) broad Black Country either but knew what an 'ommer (hammer) was and what "yo gooin'" (are you going down the pub), meant, the same as "bostin, our kid" in answer to how are you. I love "it's gone black over Bill's mother's", meaning it's probably going to rain.

The last saying, supposed to be a reference to William (Bill) Shakespeare and Stratford, but I doubt it, but it's good Black Country blarney.

The history of the place of my birth was instilled in me, from *County Express* working days, and learning from *County* reporter, Jack Haden, an exquisite doyen of Stourbridge history, and culture and prolific author of the area, including fine tomes on the Stourbridge glass industry. His erudition and learning did rub off on a young man, trying to learn journalism and understand his roots.

But also mixing with society across the board, it has to be said, in working class pubs, where Jack would not have felt much at ease, like the one at the top of our Amblecote Road and Delph Road, the Bull and Bladder, proper name The Vine, although it was never called that. The home of strong, locally produced Bathams Bitter known as perhaps the best beer, bar none in the country. Renowned with its quote from William Shakespeare's words across its top: "Blessing of your heart you brew good ale" from *The Two Gentleman of Verona*. There, you see, you can learn much from pubs, even from what's written on them!

There was another "learning" in their too, albeit a risky one, if too much ale was taken, and I too have seen men taken to this haven and not being wary enough of its strong ale, losing their legs when hitting the night air. It was a tough pub, I remember the landlord had his glasses taped together on one side with Elastoplast for what seemed years!

Warwick's in Brierley Hill High Street was another watering hole of mesmerising learning, if you would listen. More of that in the book later. Then on down to Netherton and Ma Pardoe's, where beer was brewed on the premises and the counter was the prettiest of them all, with an ultra-clean shining copper top which ran the length of the bar. Just across from the road where the anchor chain for the ill-fated Titanic ocean liner was forged. The trick with Pardoe's, or any other home brewery, was to look carefully at what the old boys in the bar were drinking before you ordered your pint of bitter! If they were not drinking "the brew" then choose something else. Sometimes, if it was a bit cloudy, it could do things to your innards that you didn't want it to do!

And working in Stourbridge, Brierley Hill, etc. as a newspaper reporter and visiting hot spots of Black

Country, like Lye, Netherton, Dudley, felt still like I was learning as a local man, as I grew up from schoolboy, teenager to adult.

We had our own accent, and although I agree mine was not of a heavy characteristic one, people knew where you came from, and we, of course, had separate identity from our Warwickshire friends in Birmingham, who had a *very* different accent to our own!

In Amblecote there were the inimitable "cuts", the canals, the very heartbeat of the Black Country before the railways came. We had a canal at the bottom of Stourbridge Town, later joined by the huge railway goods yard, we had the canal just above the bridge towards Brierley Hill, all of which carried the commerce of the area; its coal, its iron and more carefully, I suggest, our precious cut glass products. We too had our own brickworks, where the local brick made our churches, plus railways, a town gas works which stank, iron works, clay pits, leather tanning, which also stank as quite often did the "cut". So, I say I am a Black Countryman and proud of it.

My own father's mum worked at the brickworks and tough those women were too. And my grandfather, Billy, helped make some of the finest cut glass in the world, all from factories in Amblecote, Wordsley, Stourbridge and Brierley Hill.

Glassmaking had been introduced into the area in the 17th century. Made from silica (from sandstone), coal and clay, the area had all those natural products in abundance. Stourbridge fireclay was the best in the world to withstand the enormous high temperatures needed to make the glass.

For centuries "Stourbridge" glass was the finest made in the world; hand-made cut glass, not the moulded stuff in use today. From crystal, and cameo glass, it has graced the finest tables and houses everywhere.

Just for good measure, the first steam locomotive to run in America was made in Stourbridge! The Stourbridge Lion was transported to the USA in 1829. It was manufactured by the company Foster, Rastrick and Company.

But my old friend, John Hipkiss, from his roots in Netherton and Halesowen, says Amblecote was "too posh" was not the "real" Black Country, in his opinion. But I stick to my opinion too, I reckon I am close enough to be called a Black Countryman, and I loved working among these lovely people for many years in Brierley Hill, Dudley, Kingswinford, Wordsley, the Lye, Netherton, and others.

And I continued to visit the area, most weekends, for years and years, up to the late 90s, visiting my parents as they grew older and weaker, still in their same Amblecote house. The abode less appealing by then, I admit, but it "saw them out", and for that I was most grateful, among Black Country friends.

While I was writing this book, my friend John Hunter's wife, Tricia, asked if she could "do" our family tree as a winter project, as she was a learned genealogist. I agreed and Tricia soon came up with some gems from the past from the ancestor tree of our paternal side.

Family history now includes evidence of ancestors from Pensnett, Kingswinford, Sedgley, Coseley, Dudley, and Woodsetton. Names that go back to the 18th century now and this just on our dad's side. Trades include colliers, nailers, brickmakers, watermen, puddlers, blacksmiths and many early glassmakers.

This makes me solidly a Black Countryman, I contend, more than ever, with my history going back to at least 1784 in Kingswinford.. I rest my case, m'lord.

# CHAPTER ONE

# The House That Wouldn't Fall Down

Mother was always frightened that the side of our house would fall off.

You see, the semi-detached house in Amblecote, in the Midlands' historic Black Country had a great big bulge in it, caused by the clay soil under it and, I presume, lack of substantial footings that it should have been built on.

The troubling bulge was high up above the front door and as the years went by, it remained, always a worry to my mother, quite rightly, but it did not produce cracks in the brickwork somehow; and the downstairs lounge windowsill was wonky too, one corner quite a lot lower than the other end of the window. Most of the door frames were bowed so the doors didn't latch properly either.

But, luckily, the house did not fall down and even survived the best attempts of a runaway lorry to demolish it, many years later, as it crashed through our

The Edwards' family in the Amblecote garden.
Left: brother Dave and me, in front Mum and Dad.

garden brick wall, a telegraph pole and the cast iron post box on it into the front garden, missing the front of the house by inches!

The runaway Murphy's open cast coal lorry lost its brakes on the way down the hill in 1963. The terrified driver jumped out to save his life and the driverless machine gathered speed and smashed into the small front garden one morning, waking me up in the bedroom above and I shouted to my elder brother that a lorry was in the front garden.

Not much response at first from him, thinking perhaps it was a prank, although not April 1st. Our grandad, who was asleep in the front room downstairs would have taken the brunt of the catastrophe, I reckon, if it had gone forward a few more inches and smashed the window and its frame.

The item made *The Stourbridge County Express*, which published a dramatic photo of the lorry buried in the garden and my ever-stoic grandad was also in the picture, hands in pockets, explaining to the astonished neighbours what had happened that early morning.

But it remained the family home at 41 Vicarage Road, seeing my parents through to their diamond wedding, and beyond, having raised their two boys, my brother and I, in the two-bedroomed house along with my grandad, Billy Hicks, my mother's father, throughout their married life.

So, you can image it was a bit cramped for living space, but nothing like the tales my mum told me of earlier Black Country days of friend's homes where their children "top and tailed" in a bed to sleep, with one child's head one way and another child right next to them with feet next to the head. And first up got the best shoes. Seven children, my mum said.

I was born in the house in the front bedroom just after the war ended, on November 9, 1945, a Saturday it was, and although of great importance, well, to me anyway, and my mum and dad and the rest of the small family, I expect, nothing compared to the start of the Nuremberg trials later that month against Nazi war criminals and for the founding of UNESCO. And just two months earlier, Britain had ended press censorship, which was in a way fitting for me as it turned out, who made journalism his life's work.

My brother, Dave, was born just before the war started in 1938, so my parents were desperate he should not be an only child, hence my arrival. They were considering adopting until I came along. My parents and the wonky house raised and protected me for my formative years, well, up to 28, really, when I left the happy abode for far flung Northamptonshire for a new job, new life, new adventures.

The house still stands decades after it was sold to a kindly builder after the deaths of my parents and has undergone many changes. Number 41 was called "Burwood"; no one seems to know why, before Grandad bought it for cash, apparently, and is in a mixed area of private and council housing, opposite a grand old vicarage which stood in its own grounds on a slight hill looking down on us in our house. Long since demolished, it now forms Queens Crescent, but I remember it being large and foreboding to me as a child.

The busy Corbett Hospital was a few hundred yards "down" the road, built by the Stourbridge philanthropist John Corbett, known as the "Salt King". He made his millions from extracting brine to make salt in his works in Droitwich.

The church was on the opposite side, unusually made of local firebricks, not stone. It faced the Royal Oak pub, a symmetry of "good and evil" sometimes, perhaps? Make up your own minds.

In the same vicinity is the War Memorial Ground, where Stourbridge FC played as the "Glassboys", a nod to the glassmaking history of the Amblecote and Stourbridge towns. I doubt there is another football club with that nickname. Stourbridge cricket club played at the ground in the summer too, when the open side decking for the football club was taken up. Worcestershire County games were staged too, and I saw many a hero of the summer game including the likes of Tom Graveney, an imperious batsman and I can still see his cover drives to this day. Beautiful.

Before that, my own father, Stanley, a keen runner, ran in organised events on the cinder track built round the ground, first with the Stourbridge British Legion, then Harriers and later with the Stourbridge and Birchfield Harriers.

"Up" the road from our house was a bridge where happily I stood as a child getting face smudges from the dirty steam trains pulling coal waggons, and getting told off by my mother for it. A bit further on, acres of scrubby farmland, my playground and my brother's before me; but a dodgy one as the land had been mined for clay and poor-quality coal. Mine shafts just 10 feet from the surface opened up in the fields, sometimes taking down a poor cow, and a tractor and its driver once nearly toppled in.

London boys had their bomb sites; we had our own unstable arable playgrounds, without the shrapnel.

# CHAPTER TWO

# Huge Holes in
the Countryside

Amblecote Hall was known in Norman times, but the Gittins family lived in it 'til 1952. And what happened to it? You guessed it; it was demolished due to mining subsidence. The farm, our playground, went to in the most jaw-dropping way. It was open cast mined for coal in the mid-1960s and the hole in the ground left by the mine was just enormous.

The yellow tractors with tyres higher than a man, were like Dinky toys when you dared poke your head over the edge of the monstrous ravine to look at the very bottom. Awesome. But now even more dangerous, and well off-limits.

Later, with the low-quality coal burning away in power stations – the only way to burn the stuff apparently – the hole was "back-filled" with millions of tons of earth and houses were built on a new, big estate. I wonder if the new owners ever knew what a huge hole their houses had been built on!

Instead of a wiggly, subsiding narrow lane from Amblecote leading past the Birch Tree Public House towards Brierley Hill, a new, less wiggly ribbon of tarmac was laid for faster, safer access. Too fast for one car, a Jenson sports car crashed upside down with a young lad unhurt standing alongside, who would have to tell his father that he'd demolished his car!

Amblecote was originally in Staffordshire as an urban district, but in 1966 the land on the other side of the bridge became part of Brierley Hill and Dudley, while our house went into the Stourbridge area. At some time, they also changed the county boundary too, with land below our bridge becoming Worcestershire, instead of Staffs. It's still the same place, despite how many changes like that are made.

I became a reporter for the local *County Express* newspaper based in Stourbridge and one of my early jobs as a trainee journalist was covering the old, defunct urban district council meetings.

It was the best doddle of a job you could ever cover. Meetings were so well organised that the councillors met at 7.30pm and, after business and matters arising had been completed, it was 7.35 or 7.40pm and home we all went. These councillors, bless them, did not feel the need to feed their egos. Unlike many councils with elected members, which I cursed later on, who droned on and on, to get their names in the local paper. But all that is another story, for later.

Under the Local Government Act of 1974, the year after I had left the area, a new regime took over with Amblecote belonging to the Dudley Metropolitan Borough in the new West Midlands County. That was to be my last year as a resident of "Amblecote-shire".

# CHAPTER THREE

# My Parents' Wedding

My father and mother were married on September 7, 1935 at St James' Church, Wollaston, near Stourbridge. His occupation was put down on the marriage certificate as clerk, and Mum's, a table-hand, a printer, in Marks's bookshop (in High Street, Stourbridge). Dad's father, Richard Edwards, was a blacksmith, making iron fences and Mum's father, a glassmaker.

Dad's address was 14 Studley Gate, Stourbridge and Mum's, 99 High Street, Wollaston.

Luckily, the documents relating to the organisation of the wedding day still survive. The hire of a car for the wedding, costing £1 and 10 shillings (£1.50), and was provided by Vanns' Service Garage, unhappily the make of car is not given!

Vanns' provided a private car hire service, from Oldswinford, near Stourbridge, and was open on Sundays. They did repairs and complete overhauls, could supply any make of car, took deferred payments, had car storage facilities, a car valeting service, accumulator charging (for radios, I presume).

Mum and Dad on their wedding day in 1935, St James Church, Wollaston, near Stourbridge.

At £1 5s 6d (£1.27), almost the same as the car hire, the flowers were from C Layland, nurseryman and florist of Bright Street, Wollaston, near Stourbridge. Mum had a bouquet for 10s 6d, two other bouquets at five shillings each, four buttonholes – two shillings – and chrysanths at three shillings.

The drinks were supplied by Hill and Reading, grocers and wine merchants of 141 High Street, Stourbridge, which was still in business in my time in Stourbridge years later. The order included two bottles of port – seven shillings – two bottles of sherry, also seven shillings, one dozen grapefruit, 2s 6d, two dozen bottles (of beer?), 2s. Total; £1 and 1 shilling (£1.05).

GT Coxhill, caterers and confectioners of 47 High Street, Stourbridge wrote Mum a letter on August 23, 1935, which read:

*Dear Miss, Many thanks for your kind enquiry re-wedding breakfast for 25-30 guests. We shall be delighted to wait upon you and I submit a specimen menu for your consideration. We are always pleased to alter or submit other suggestions, if you so desire.*

*May we also add that our goods are the highest quality in every respect. Assuring you always of my best attention, believe this.*

*Menu. Cold ham, cold ox tongue, green salad, mayonnaise, rolls and butter. Wine trifle jellies. Meringues and cream (fresh). Assorted biscuits. Cheese, rolls, butter and biscuits, coffee, lemonade. Full service, etc, flowers, lemon chrysanths. Glasses for lemonade, plus waitresses. Any kind of glasses and tables, these items will be at a slightly increased charge. Inclusive price 3s 9d per head.*

I reckon the total in today's money would have been nearly £700 for the car hire, flowers, drinks, and wedding breakfast.

All went without a hitch but they made one mistake after the wedding. They missed the train on the way to their honeymoon – Mum swore they were both sober – which was to be spent at Babbacombe, near Torquay!

The only seaside Mum had seen up to then was Weston. A telegram was sent to the boarding house and they arrived much later than expected, at midnight. Knocking the door my father said, 'I am so sorry to be so late, but we were married this morning and we missed the train.' Mum didn't mind the attention that brought, but Dad suffered for not keeping his mouth shut!

But four years of idyllic family life for my parents was to change forever, like it did for the whole country, when war was declared in 1939. Brother David was just 10 months old when war started. You can only try to imagine the horrors young mums went through trying to bring up young babies with all the rationing and concerns for safety it brought.

Normality was sought for the family unit, although "holidays" were very difficult, but the family did manage the odd week at nearby Bridgnorth, nowhere near the dangerous coast, but at least it had the beautiful River Severn flowing through the magnificent town. Close seaside resort trips were somehow managed towards the end of the war too.

Father was in a reserved occupation during the war, working in the steel works of Bayliss Jones and Bayliss, Wolverhampton. He was an estimator, but was asked to stay on as a workman to help the war effort. His war was at home and Mother thanked God every day for their being together, but come the evening after work he had to go out again as part of the Air Raid Precautions (ARP) for fire watching. This was particularly for the deadly incendiary bombs which set light to buildings after the other bombs had done their worst. Not much sleep for a working man while son David and Mum tried to keep safe in the air raid shelter in the garden.

He said very little to me about the war, but I do remember he told me he went into a building, which had been bombed and found what looked like an old-fashioned stove pipe sticking up, before realising it was an unexploded bomb and had to help evacuate the area for safety. Uncertain times for Mum, Dad and my brother, David, as it was for millions of British people wondering how and if they were to survive a world war.

Our only consolation was the fact that Dad didn't have to go away to fight like millions of others; his fight was spent on the home front. There were many casualties among those men trying to keep us safe; it was not all like its portrayed in the *Dad's Army* comedy series.

Mum and Dad on honeymoon in 1935, Babbacombe,
Devon. Taken by a street photographer, remember them?

Amblecote was under threat, because of its close proximity to the industrial areas of Birmingham, Wolverhampton and Coventry. Dad said he could see the orange glow in the sky while on fire watching duties the nights when Coventry was raised to the ground by the bombers. Having a young baby during war time must have been frightening for any young family at that terrible time in history.

David must have been a contended baby as he had a crib in the Andersson shelter erected in the garden by Dad and neighbours when the bomb attacks were on, and slept through most of the noise most nights!

# CHAPTER FOUR

# The Children, Andrew and David

Luckily, the family coped, and survived the war unscathed.

Mum and Dad's old pedal bikes were still used after the war with trips into the countryside around beauty spots like Kinver and Clent with David in tow too this time around.

Seriously thinking of adoption after six years and after a "small" operation, Mum had me, Andrew. So now the family was four, five counting her old dad. There was a bit more of the pulling in of the belt to keep the yearly holidays going, said Mum.

I have no revelations of being able to remember things that happened to me in my pram aged six months as other people seem to be able to recount! Later on, I do have memories of a very happy, contented childhood.

At about five, I must have been a bit of a rebel, as I insisted on wearing a sheath knife in my belt when I went out with Mum. Other mums were aghast, but

Mum took it in her stride and said it would be OK, which it was.

A weekly visit to the Co-op in Brettell Lane, walking through the grounds of the Corbett hospital with its imposing gates, past the Fish Inn, now gone, past the Little Pig public house and on up the road on the way to Wordsley, to the shop. Clutching her "divvy", Mum did her weekly shop but what was a treat to me was being able to look at the system used in the shop for collecting the money and giving out change to the customers.

"We Edwards" is Mum's caption from our holiday in 1953, Kewstoke Woods, Weston. From left: Dave, Dad and Mum and me. Those spilled blackberries we'd collected had something to do with me I'm afraid!

A system of pneumatic tubes on the counters had small cylinders running in them. The shop assistant put the money in a cylinder, say a pound note, then placed it in the tube system which sent it whooshing up to a central "money room" in which the pound was taken out, replaced with the correct change and whooshed down to the counter assistant who opened the canister and gave the customers their change.

At my young age, I'd never seen anything so modern, so up-to-date, so space-age, and I remained enthralled with it for ages. On its own, it was worth the long walk at my mother's side, protecting her with my knife on my belt. Brother Dave had similar memories of the pneumatic tubes in a shop in Stourbridge.

We had a decent sized garden which turned into anything we children wanted it to be, like all children. We dressed up as cowboys and Indians, had tents in which various childhood fantasies were played out. I don't remember too many friends' names, but friends there were who came round to play along with me.

I do remember, one door down from us, I got on extremely well with my friend, Nigel, who was mixed race, with an English mum and a West Indian father. The cooking smells emanating from their house from what, for us, was "exotic" food then, were magic, very new to our community.

The closest I got to serious injury as a youngster was because of my own stupidity, and my brother. He was chopping wood with an axe – seven years older, remember – and I walked behind him, not in front, just as he brought the axe over his head and the blunt end hit me on my head, causing a bloody wound. I can't remember going anywhere to have the wound dressed but I must have, but the worst aspect was, when I went to school, they insisted I keep my school cap on at all times, for hygiene, I suppose. Very embarrassing.

I do remember a hospital visit to remove a ball of silver paper which I had stuffed up my nose, as you do.

Enville Street School, Stourbridge was my first place of learning. I believe I was in a school play, got stage fright or something and missed out pages and pages of the script, making the whole thing nonsense. It could have been when I was "acting" as the father in a christening. I was never asked to tread the boards again and I never volunteered.

Ever onwards in my education, after failing my eleven-plus exam, I moved to Longlands Comprehensive School, Stourbridge. What a ridiculous system that was, trying to map out a child's education at the age of 11, and sending them to either comprehensive or grammar school, as was the choice at the time. I didn't have a clue, perhaps I was a slow learner, scholastically, or something, but 11 was simply too young for me to get stuck into education, although my parents were very supportive and wanted my brother and I to have the best education we could get, which they knew was vital for our long-term futures.

Brother Dave had more of the academic brains in our family; he went to the King Edward VI Grammar School in the town, went through further education, gaining professional qualifications.

I was happy at the comprehensive, and two years later, I sat for the thirteen-plus exam, which had been introduced to catch those who had just missed out on a perceived higher academic path in grammar school education. Pass it I did, I say pass, I scraped in. The headmaster, Mr R L Chambers (Chamber Pot to the pupils, of course), petrifying in his black gown and mortar board hat, interviewed me. Or interrogated me.

I had a very poor result in the maths section and I promised to improve, so they let me in. I've always wondered if my brother, having been a pupil before me, helped me get a place. I never got a grasp of mathematics, which to this day remains a fog, a closed book.

It didn't help me that I had what I thought of as a bully of a maths teacher either, who used to bellow – that's my recollection, especially in the afternoons. Even then, I thought I knew why it happened after lunch. He'd yell, 'Do you understand, Edwards, do you understand?' Frightened to say I didn't understand what I'd been asked to study, I said yes. So, I never learning anything because I hadn't understood the basics of what I was being asked in the first place.

But English language and especially literature was a different thing altogether. I thought they came easy to me, easier than maths anyway, and I enjoyed them, so did okay. I had two years of a comprehensive education where woodworking and metalworking were on the agenda – more hands-on things.

Woodwork was on the schedule at the grammar school, but I didn't like that, as the teacher used to throw mallets at pupils, always missing of course, he must have had a good aim. Then there were the teachers who threw blackboard rubbers across the classroom, and one who used to hit children on the bottom with a size 10 plimsoll. The cane was still in use for serious crimes, across the palms of the hands or on the bottom.

I think children were bad too, but not to the extent of hitting them. Thank goodness for some changes. But putting chalk or some chemical into the inkwells, which foamed up brilliantly, was great fun and caused uproar before detentions. Yes, we had inkwells and pens to write with in those days, wow.

One teacher, who was in charge for art, was an easy target for the naughty boys, who would soak his gown with paint thrown on by their paint brushes as he walked down the aisles between the desks. He never seemed to notice. He must have, of course, at the end of lessons, but it was never mentioned. I think he just gave up. We heard that one teacher was on leave, suffering a nervous breakdown, but not the art man.

The Stourbridge Grammar was for those destined to be academic scholars, particularly in Latin and Greek, on to Oxbridge and all that, and I knew it was not going to be me. I was a member of the non-academic branch of the school, ending up in the sixth form in Six C. Six for Commercial Stream. I was surprised to learn that brother, Dave, had also been in 6C before me for a few weeks! We weren't even put in for our A levels, that was our level, pardon the pun!

I quite liked it, got on well with it. We had typing lessons from the headmaster's secretary, Miss Bunn, and I passed exams in touch typing and got a good speed too, plus a bit of shorthand.

There was what we'd call today "media studies" too, where a very calm and brilliant teacher, the deputy head I think, taught us about newspapers, the media and carefully explained their contents, how to understand them, their opinion columns, etc. It couldn't have been better for me, as my career, my life, was destined to be in newspapers; how lucky was that, I had a head start!

One master, gave me my first insight into music, also a passion I had for the rest of my life. I will always be indebted to him. Not only did he bring in classical records for us to listen to, which was great – anything was better than sitting at a desk doing maths – he brought in his own jazz records too. We listened to Count Basie, Duke Ellington, Louis Armstrong, all sorts of great music. I remember to this day that the Buddy Rich Big Band made a big impression on me and I was over the moon when I saw them play a very loud gig in Birmingham's Odeon Theatre years later. We listened while he talked enthusiastically about all sorts of music and I was hooked forever, enjoying jazz, blues, rock, folk, and classical. Wish I could remember his name. But I can't. Forgive me.

I don't think Robert Plant, a fellow pupil of the grammar school at the same time as me, ever came to these sessions, but he too was having his own epiphany in music. He became part of supergroup Led Zeppelin.

Even getting expelled didn't hold Robert up! He was on a mission, knew what he wanted, although apparently Mr Chambers told him he would never make anything of himself.

He probably changed his mind when Robert, in later life, knocked on the door of the headmaster's home to show him his first Rolls Royce, which he'd just bought. That was it really, not showing off, but just to prove a point. Just to prove the headmaster had been wrong about his former pupil.

Star and rock god status didn't happen overnight of course, and my late friend, Gareth Morgan, who was a "friend" of Robert during those early days, remembered when they chased each other in rival gangs up Stourbridge High Street, squabbling over some girl or another they both wanted to get acquainted with. He was a "grammar grub", you see, and Gareth was from the Bluecoat School.

Gareth remembered what he said was Robert's first gig; back of the Stourbridge Bus Garage, in a back room of a pub, when Robert and his very young "musicians" were booed off the stage because none of them had yet learnt to play or sing much, and had to leg it as the "crowd" got angry!

Changing the mood somewhat, I was also proud to say I had gone to the same school as Robert Plant, but a few centuries before, Samuel Johnson, one of the greatest English poets, playwrights and biographers, attended the King Edward VI Grammar School. Johnson

(1709-1784) spent around six months at the school aged about 16. The school was founded in 1430 and the charter for the grammar school was granted in 1552 by King Edward VI. In 1755, Johnson wrote *A Dictionary of the English Language*, which came 150 years before the *Oxford English Dictionary*. Simply an amazingly talented man and he too is an old boy of Stourbridge Grammar, well, for sixth months anyway. I was shown a very old desk with "SJ" cut into it and was told Johnson sat at it, but I don't believe it could have been that old, and I was very sceptical.

## CHAPTER FIVE

# All Boys Together!

KEGS, as it was called, was an all-boys school in those far off days, which made me awkward around the opposite sex for a while. But I got over it. I also got over playing rugby, as scrum half, because I was so small, only at a very low level when I couldn't get out of it. I remember we used to play a kind of hockey, "shinty" or something, for those who did not like rugger. That was even more brutal than rugby. You really had to watch your shins from the hard ball or flailing wooden sticks struck at you fiercely by the opposition. Football was never played or mentioned at the school.

One good game was great fun. We played "fives" against the bike shed wall in the playground. It was like an early game of squash, I suppose, with just one wall in play. Using a tennis ball, there were two players and you had to whack the ball into the wall with the palm of your hand over a chalk mark "net" then the other player tried to retrieve it for rallies. Exciting. The bike sheds were where the smokers tried to hide themselves away for a drag of the weed, but I think they were always caught. Teachers weren't that stupid and knew where to look!

With my big brother Dave on hols, destination unknown, with bucket and spade.

We had to wear a uniform, green blazer and cap and woe betide you if a dreaded "police" prefect caught you in town without your cap on. The school was an imposing pile from the front, but our way in from the back entrance led to an abattoir and a leather tanning yard next to the "cut" (canal). I had to walk past this smelly leather place each day, it was simply horrendous some days, and the foam was sometimes yards thick and flew about on windy days. Yuck.

I used to walk to school in the morning, return home for lunch (no school meals for me), walk back for the afternoon lessons and back home in the evening. I reckon the walk was about a mile, maybe slightly under, each time. The route from home was via, in part, an unmade lane called Gas Lane. Named because, at its Lower High Street, Stourbridge end, it went past the Town Gas works, with its ever-present smell of sulphur, a by-product of making gas from coke. Some folk apparently thought the smell of sulphur in the atmosphere was good for children's health, curing asthma, colds, and I was told parents took their kids for a sniff or two. Maybe true, or not!

But my shortcut to the rear entrance of the school took a left off Gas Lane, over a big iron trestle bridge with wooden steps, which went over the railway shunting yards where steam trains moved industrial cargoes around in waggons.

On the other side of the bridge there was the canal and the leather tanning works. You didn't want to breathe that atmosphere in more than you could avoid and your step became more hurried to get out of it on bad days. Workers were trapped in that works of course, five or six days a week cleaning out cow hides. What a job. A few more steps took me into the school playground.

I grew up, industry all around with its various smells. The crystal glass factories pushing out lead-infused fumes from its tall cone-shaped chimneys above the hot kilns (hence the name lead crystal), Town Gas Works, leather tanning and the smell of the "cut"; not pleasant to be near on hot days with the water an unpleasant colour of brown and dirty. I definitely breathed my fair share of Black Country air.

At school we took our exercise in this "fresh" air. Everyone had to put their name down for athletics and I always chose the three shortest disciplines to make my early exit as I wasn't that keen; the 100 yards, the high jump and hop step and jump (now the triple jump) which was funny because I was quite small for my age and not really built for huge strides or leaping high into the air! I did enjoy the technique of the triple jump and I thought I got quite good at it. For my age and size anyway.

At home things were physically tight. Dave and I had one bedroom, parents had the other, with Grandad having a bedsit in the front room downstairs; remember, it was only a tiny two-bedroomed house.

This gave various factions in the house to mostly rub along, but not always. There were rifts between Dad and Grandad for a start, sometimes not even speaking!

Mum in the middle, of course, trying to keep the peace. Her advice for keeping the peace was, 'I shall get no golden crown in heaven for this, it was my duty, but, if it is worth anything, here is my advice to people about to undertake the same necessary step (having husband, her father and two children in one house). Exceptionally good manners by all, or a huge house where everyone can at least be alone sometimes.' She was not granted a big house all her married life and my mother was a saint of a woman who, most times, kept her cool, but "damn, blast and bugger it" did come out a few times, as a safety valve! To herself, I have to add, in pure frustration.

A bigger house did come up for sale in the same road and Mum would have loved it, but Dad, being careful, thought it would be a step too far financially and did not agree with the move. She did not get her bigger house, which would have made her life much happier with the extra space. She never forgave him for that particular decision.

# CHAPTER SIX

# Sporting Interests

Mum and Dad's safety valve from the presence of Grandad was tennis. Weekly tennis sessions were a godsend for Mum and Dad to get out of the house, have some R & R, as it would be called now, and exercise and have a jolly good laugh with their friends, Lil and Eric, who had a tandem.

They weren't in any posh club, oh no, they booked three hours sessions in the public parks twice a week for years. Bicycles were used by three of the party – Dad and Lil and Eric – while Mum and I had to catch the "erratic" bus to join them for the session in the park.

It was the start of a passion of sport for me, all brought about by my parents' love of tennis. My elder brother, with the gap of seven years between us, which always seemed a big one for me growing up, had no love of tennis. He enjoyed scouting, which I tried, but I found out I was never one to join a club or a group, not much anyway, always having to find my own way in life, which was not always a good thing. But I was not a "joiner-in" of a lot of things.

Stambermill church hall, badminton club, near Lye in the 1960s. Second left back row: great family friend Eric Nash. Middle row, second left: Eric's wife, Lil, who had the best laugh I've ever heard. Note the low ceiling, not ideal for badminton!

For Dave, scouting and, later on, camping, gave him a lifelong love of the outdoors, which took him to all the great hills and mountains of Great Britain and, later on, Europe, then Australia, and America.

But I was sport mad like Mother and Father and towed along to the uneven grass courts, nothing like Wimbledon, I'm afraid, but good enough for us. Mum said, 'Andrew was satisfied as long as the last half an hour was given over to him (to have a game). He had a dad who taught him the game correctly and he would play with a full-sized racket. He was good, too. My 40s were my happiest years and continued later at a church club. We did enjoy club company, but somehow, it was incomparable with the two weekly park dates. At 45, I was learning badminton. This being the sport for the younger one, who took to it straight away.'

I found I was more suited to badminton, I found it quicker and more demanding and it became my sport of choice for many years. I was not a natural, as my friend, Martin Hill, was, but I had to try hard to attain better standards, which eventually brought me up to Worcestershire County standards, and an enjoyable time as county third team captain and, on some occasions, a spell in the second team as well.

My grounding in the sport came first at Stambermill church hall, just down the road from Lye, just outside Stourbridge. It was not an ideal venue for badminton as it had a very low roof, whereas badminton should be played with a high ceiling. So low was Stambermill's ceiling and hanging lights that a tall, athletic player could leap up and smash the light fittings to bits with a racket. It didn't do the rackets much good either. I saw this on a couple of occasions, once by Ralph Thomson, the Lye Town football goalkeeper, so quite a big, tough chap. Low ceiling made for an interesting, fast-paced game with no high clearances on the cards to get out of trouble and regroup.

When Mum played in the local church halls, and I followed, it was a time-consuming task for club members to remove all the church chairs and the odd table from the hall space, to become the court, put the net up, etc., and, after the night had finished, put everything back again each week! We were all keen.

Later, as a teenager, I joined Stourbridge Institute badminton club, a purpose-built court in an impressive club with seven snooker tables on the ground floor. For many years, until I left the area in 1973, it was my life, playing badminton maybe three or four times a week. Mum constantly having to wash my white shorts, shirts and socks with never a murmur. Rackets were state of the art as we progressed up the ladder, getting hold of special lightened Maurice Robinson Dunlop Maxplys, or, my favourites, Silver Greys, made in Cambridge.

We were a successful club in the area and the Institute were among the top dogs in the Cradley Heath Churches League and the Worcestershire leagues for season after season. I still have the Worcestershire Boys Doubles trophy which I won, with Martin Hill, I think, from 1962.

It was a wonderful time in my life and I progressed in the Institute club as its captain in the men's and mixed doubles teams and was one of the selectors of the teams too. It was a great honour and a great regret to me that, after being selected to be a member of the county selection committee, I had to resign without taking up the post as I was about to move out of the area. I would have liked to have given something back to the sport which gave me so much for so many years.

I did play against many top players, including Gillian Gilks, who played for the Barnt Green club, near Bromsgrove *and* England and Great Britain. Gillian, for a start, won 11 titles at the All-England championships at Wembley, in singles, women's doubles and mixed doubles. It was the world championship of badminton at the time. At interval time in our match in the Worcestershire league, she made us tea. Wow, I've never forgotten that. She was lovely.

We regularly played against men's doubles pair, George Cartwright and Rob Lewis, in the Worcester league too and they used to qualify for the All-England Championships, which was a great feat. They used to toy with us when we played them, before smashing us off the court as and when they wanted! Exhausting. I remember we played against David and Ian Eddy of Staffordshire and England. Always on the losing side, of course. Martin Hill and I were then being asked to attend coaching sessions for Staffordshire County badminton, a great honour.

I did help one young woman, Sue Asman, later Robinson, to reach her goal in the sport. Sue was a wonderfully talented Worcestershire County tennis player, but came to the Stourbridge Institute to play badminton for us as a novice and I taught her one or two rudimentary techniques of the game, which were different to tennis. She was a very quick learner and was the strongest lady player I ever met. She could hit a round arm backhand "tennis" shot from the back of the court and hit the shuttlecock six feet up the wall on the far side of the court when she started to learn.

Sue played for us for many successful seasons and among the honours she gained was becoming Worcestershire County Ladies Singles champion, a very high standard. I'm glad I helped her hone her early considerable skills.

# CHAPTER SEVEN

# Mum Becomes a Teacher!

My mother was asked by a local private school who were short of a part-time games mistress to help them out! This was a lady who had left school at 14, so had very basic education, no fault of hers, of course, that was how it had been in those years.

She said yes, and had three or four years of very pleasant interaction with children who she loved anyway. She had to wrestle with her conscience as she had staunch views of "paying parents", as she called them, being entitled to the best for their children in private education.

Still, it was a temporary appointment, and I believe something of a lifesaver for her mental health as it enabled her to get out of the house for an hour or two. I expect she was really good at it; anyone could blow a little whistle for netball, she said, then she arranged tennis matches with other schools, and organised swimming lessons at the baths, and other sporting aspirations for the good of the pupils. Aspirations that had been closed for her all her life.

My favourite photo of Mum. She was about 16, taken at Nova Studios, situated over Woolworth's in Stourbridge.

'Now in my later life, I was gaining the sport I so dearly wanted in my own youth. These children did not realise how lucky they were. It had been a long time ago since I actually had to pay to use a hall to practice gym, and that was a long time after my schooldays,' said Mum.

'It was a pity to see this school close, I had been so happy there. In my 40s, I cured everything with a racket, getting rid of pent-up emotions of life. This was saying something, as I was no longer "Little Mary" now. Even with all the exercise and keeping home for five people, I was "Big Mary" now. Not bothering about doctors, I did not realise this was the start of my life-changing thyroid problems. But it was wonderful at the time.'

Nobody deserved that period of her life more than she did when things went so right for her, as she had endured a hard early life, and ill health was to be a constant companion in her later life, unfortunately. Hardly ever did she complain. She was a saint, my mother, a saint in everything she did for us.

A little more money was coming into the house with her school job and, yes, as she said, she enjoyed living life to the full in her 40s. Both us boys were at grammar school. The youngest, me, always knowing he wanted to be a journalist, she said.

Brother Dave was different from me. 'After national service, he was lucky to be enrolled in the Royal Navy – the service always appealed to him – he did not mind about going at all,' she said.

Luckily for me, by the time I was the right age for national service, it had been abandoned, in 1960. I would have hated it and probably would have been unhealthy for me mentally. I was not the joining-in type of person, not happy to be coerced into doing something I did not want to do, so I believe I would have had to have the stuffing knocked out of me to conform to a rigid military life. Thousands upon thousands of young people had to do it. I am just happy I was not called upon to do so.

My mum added, 'Dave was stationed in Malta and learnt telecommunications. He was lucky during his service doing thousands of miles at the nation's expense and greatly appreciating it. It was part of his happy wanderlust he always had.'

After his Navy days, Dave went back to education and college for many years of hard studying, with grants and then no grant, to obtain his Institute of Electronic and Radio Engineers (IERE) qualification, working as well as studying. He left the country to become a lecturer. He travelled to Africa where he met his wife, Christine.

Mum said, 'We parents realised it would be the first of his wanderings. One has to love and let go. The Black Country was my horizon. The easier it is for all people, youth especially, to mix freely, the less reason for misunderstanding.

'In the last two wars of our generation, the average working man did not have a chance of looking and seeing or mixing with the people of other countries. If one was born in the Black Country, one died in the Black Country, and the word of government was gospel.

'If only this generation will use its knowledge and will mix and talk with all colours and creeds and so use their own reasoning, we will be half way to consistent world peace.'

Very wise, was our old mum.

# CHAPTER EIGHT

# Mum's Ill Health Strikes

Unhappily for my mum, her world was turned upside down when she was 50. With a jolt.

She had womb problems, a burst appendix and an ongoing thyroid issue, growing inwardly on a main artery in the neck. Treatment was sought immediately, but heart problems also hit her.

All sports, choral societies (she loved singing), church activities, even too much walking was too great a strain for her heart. 'So, I abided, putting my family first. All other things went overboard. Going nowhere, without help, but knowing thousands are worse off, one has to accept it. My family were the best in the world, my husband especially. We got by. Half hourly chores, and with one day per week in bed, helped by science, with its tablets daily, we managed,' said my mum stoically.

I knew she had been very badly let down by her health, it was heart-breaking. She saw positives in everything and stuck to the "God helps those who help themselves" mantra.

After ill health struck Mum, Dad passed his driving test aged 50 to help her mobility and his first car was a pre-war Morris 8, second hand from Uncle Peter. Mum posing in the driving seat, she never drove. Dad in the passenger seat, with windscreen open.

Mum and Dad had the chance of an old caravan, it even had stained glass in its little windows I recall. It was already on a tiny site only 18 miles away in the Far Forest, part of the larger Wyre Forest near Bewdley, Worcestershire.

It wasn't ever going to move again, it was not a caravan for moving, it had to stay put. Problem number one, and a big one: how to get there for important and lifesaving R & R. The family did not have a car, always relying on walking, buses, and bicycles. Dad did not even have a driving licence, so he mustered all his skills and passed his driving test first time at the age of 50, which was a fantastic achievement, I thought.

The "new" second hand Morris 1000. Proud Dad at Deganwy, north Wales, I think. Favourite destination for years, which gave me great memories and new ones on recent visits.

Second problem: find a car. It was Uncle Peter's old car which came to the family rescue, not a new one, a 1940s Morris 8, which, as Mother said, somehow matched the old caravan! Their old car had to be given rest because it regularly overheated after chuffing up long hills; it took my mum and dad to other places of pleasure as well as the caravan visits.

To her, to have an afternoon nap in the caravan, and wake up to the peace of the forest, was bliss. I know how she felt, sometimes simple pleasures in life are much the best. I have felt this all my life too. And I too had blissful times in that caravan, then walking, sometimes alone in the Far Forest, sometimes with my father, listening to the little babbling brook running through the middle of it, listening to the rustle of the wildlife as it scuttled about its daily ways, knowing wild places so much better than us. We were all just passers-by – of very little importance compared with the big end game; nature. I loved that place, still do, on very infrequent visits as I grew older, reminiscing what wonderful, peace-giving things it did for Mum and Dad. In their difficult middle and late years on this earth. I am truly, truly forever thankful.

After a late start to his motoring career, Dad replaced the ageing Morris 8, which I remember smelt wonderfully of old leather, to give Mother much more comfort and more reliability for them both. He had a couple of Morris 1000s, one reg was LRN 940, which I can still remember, for some odd reason, then another one, plus a Morris 1100. Very modern for us!

I must own up; when very young, I illegally started up the engine and crashed the first Morris into the back of the wooden garage wall, breaking the bumper in two! I was not at all popular that day! Stupid.

On the motorway, with me giving it a bit of a run (after I had passed my test, of course), the later 1100 went really quite quickly, but don't tell the old man! But BMC's indecisive gearbox operated through a long "pudding stirrer stick" gear lever, and was a constant pain.

I can't remember when he gave up driving, but he knew when he wasn't quite safe enough and said, 'That's it, I'm stopping now.' He had a very minor bump, I believe. Very sensible, very wise, was my father. He was a bit quiet sometimes, while he thought about things, worked things out, not one to make an instant decision when great thought was sometimes necessary. Wonder where I got that from?

One funny car story from the family. On one winter night, my mother and dad were going back home, from Eric and Lil's house in the Broadway, Norton when, out of the blue, she said to him, 'I think I might learn to drive.'

In a couple of miles, Dad pressed every button, both necessary and mostly unnecessary, more than once, wipers going on, then off, heater on, heater off, gear shift up, gear shift down, wiping the inside of the screen with his glove, as he knew she was watching. 'I don't think I'll bother,' said Mum at the end of the trip. Dad had done his job of putting her off driving. It was never mentioned again!

# CHAPTER NINE

# Mum's Early Days

Mum was four years old when the First World War started and times were tough. Even an egg was precious and made sandwiches for three of the Hicks family. Nell had married Billy Hicks and Mum was born 10 months later into a two-up, two-down Wollaston house, which Bill had filled with good furniture from a Wordsley family who had emigrated to Canada.

Bill had a good job in the local glass works, making wine glasses, and had learned to be exceptionally careful with money. He had been born with nothing and his dark-haired, dark-eyed sister, Mary-Ann, was to be brought up and loved, said Mum, by smashing grandparents. Their mum had to work hard in a local brick factory when her husband died of TB in his late '30s. Money was scarce and everything was shared.

Reflecting on her own mother, who sadly died so young, leaving Mum bereft of motherly love and pretty alone at 14 to look after her own father, to take his wife's place, she wrote, 'She too would have delighted to share our small caravan and car, which we had in our later years.'

The only photo we have of my Mum's Mum, Nell,
left with Mum centre and her Dad, Billy Hicks.
Mum's childhood was idyllic until Nell died at 43.

Mum as a young girl, having cycled from Stourbridge to Bridgnorth, sitting on the bridge. That's Dad's bike on the left and Mum's front wheel on right. They were avid cyclists in their youth, as were many of their generation – distance no object.

But what luxuries did Nell possess? Not a luxury, but she had her husband, her "Mare", her home and her one treasured piano. 'We know she was happy with these, but I still would have liked her to see the Far Forest, which we so loved later on in our lives, me and Stan.

'I can imagine the light shining in her pale blue eyes. It was only a few miles from her home and I doubt she knew of Far Forest's existence.

'Radio, television and twice-yearly visits to the coast, all would have been a real thrill to my mother. But she would have given it all up to see and live with her grandsons. She would have showered them with love.

'My dad lived for 30 odd years in retirement, with all those present-day facilities; TV, etc. Such a pity that Will did not have Nell's company for the later end of his life. What a wonderful gift of God to have our partners to grow old with together,' Mum said.

Instead, my own mum had to see to his daily needs for all those years as he grew ever more frail, and she looked after him right until his contented death, all the while seeing to her own husband. Life is sometimes very cruel.

Mum's much earlier memory is of crawling next door to be fussed over by the "grown-ups", only for tears to come when the door was shut and she couldn't get out. 'The very thought of being penned in and with a door knob too high to reach was too much,' she wrote.

Memories, too, of a homemade swing attached to the communal brewhouse door to keep her happy while the weekly wash was in progress. 'The old-fashioned boiler eating up all the slack and belching clouds of steam every time the big, well-scrubbed lid was removed, the busy housewives, with soap up to the elbows, pushing in the clothes.'

All children must go through it and Mum was no exception; she was taken to the photographers with her mother. 'A perfect picture of my mother, Nellie, but what made me stick my tongue out? Only a little way, but out.'

Recreation came with walks back and forth to the local beauty spots – Kinver or Clent, usually – although there were trams which passed her door in High Street, Wollaston.

Money was not wasted on "pop" (lemonade), only cold tea or water accompanied the children then, but when there were enough pennies, sweet shops were visited, usually on a Saturday as a treat, when the spoils were shared out with friends and consumed on the front step of the house, as the trams clanked by.

After the sweets, Mum and her friends had fields to play in opposite their terraced house, with children of mixed ages. 'With the little 'uns being looked after by the big 'uns,' she said.

'Clent was a big treat, and somehow pennies were found for donkey rides up the hills. If there was no money, we slid down grassy slopes instead, usually getting a slap on return home as our knickers were not robust enough to stand the strain.'

Mum was taken to collect blackberries in the autumn by her mum, always an adventure, as Nellie always seemed to get involved with flocks of sheep, bulls giving chase and farmers becoming cross at her antics, but always falling for her mother's charm.

At home Nellie set up a home fit for a king and queen. 'She was proud of her home and household. I am perfectly sure that she was touched by a fairy at birth. With the gifts of happiness, cheerfulness and utter contentment. All this with the burden of her ill-health from when I was two years old. Her years were short, 43 in all, but she still lives in her only daughter's heart.' Those years were filled with as much fun as they could possibly be. 'Seeing Father Christmas loaded with a full sack of toys coming through a big French window was bliss. A special book given to me was treasured for years. But to my dad, it meant nothing at all, just a time to get through. For 16 years we had each other's company, her sunny disposition making my whole world. Our thoughts were as one. Maybe I was a little more serious of the two, knowing that, for all Mum's pluck and sunny disposition, her life was doomed. Dad and I kept it from her that she was dying at the end. That final year gave me an old head on young shoulders. I died a death with her.' Nellie succumbed to kidney disease.

With the death of her mum, I believe Mum took great solace in music. She was always interested in music around that time and I do remember we had an upright piano in the house, a Steinway, a great manufacturer, which we gave away. I believe her dad would have paid for "Mare" to continue her passion, although perhaps a little unwillingly, as he was so careful with his money.

On Saturday December 12, 1925 at 10am, when she was 14, Mum went to Birmingham to take her music exam at Lawrence's College, 86 Corporation Street. It was a local examination in the Theory of Music, under the auspices of the Trinity College of Music, London. Her registration number was 7098. She passed the preparatory division with a score of 89 out of 100. You needed at least 60 marks for a pass. For notation, she gained 23 out of a possible 25, for time, also 23, for scale 24, and for terms 19.

The following year, in June, 1926, Mum gained her pupil's certificate from the Trinity College of Music, junior division in the theory of music at the local examination in Birmingham.

I can only imagine the trepidation of a young girl travelling from the Black Country to the city of Birmingham for an exam. Very daunting, I would have thought. Did Dad go with her, because he rarely went anywhere on a bus or a train? We shall never know.

I have my own memories of Mum's piano-playing when I was growing up as a child. There were piano sessions when she would read the musical scores of show tunes of the day, like *The White Horse Inn*, which Dad and I could try to sing along to. More popular tunes, really, not classical. Mum could read any sheet of music put in front of her, but never played anything without it in front of her. I remember her playing everything with gusto with wrists cocked correctly in the air, with fingers outstretched ready for action. I found a violin in the house after Dad died, but I have no recollection of him every trying to play it. Perhaps he did before I was born, I simply do not know.

It is one great regret that I was afforded piano lessons by my mum, but stupidly threw away the chance. Sometimes we are too stupid for words as we grow up. Yet music always remained a passion with me all my life and to have been able to play piano or something else always eluded me.

One favourite musical story of Mum's, was when she was cajoled to play the church organ because they knew she played piano. She was a member of Amblecote Parish Church Mothers' Union group and they found themselves without an organist for a public event in the church, but I don't remember what it was.

It was an old organ, with those huge pipes, etc., and some sort of pedal arrangement on the floor too, as well as rows of keys, many more than her normal piano keyboard of one set of black and white keys. Mum tried her best and pulled out just enough stops to make it work, not daring to put her feet on the floor under her chair as she didn't know what those pedals did.

Unfortunately for her, the little stool or seat she was sat on started to move backwards during her performance and she was getting further and further away from the keyboard as the piece continued! So, she was at full stretch at the end, almost falling forward with hands outstretched, still playing! Like a Monty Python sketch. She got away with it though. Very brave. Bless her.

# CHAPTER TEN

# My Own *Stourbridge County Express* Days

Now I fast forward in my own life. I always knew what I wanted to do for a job, my profession. I wanted to be a journalist. I was leaving school, with a few O levels, and typewriting skills, which were unusual for a lad, that was it really.

I had always read *Motor Sport* and the wonderful writing of its editor, Bill Boddy, and the magazine's continental correspondent, Dennis Jenkinson (also known as DSJ) who eschewed planes in favour of visiting European Grand Prix races in a Jaguar E-Type. Who could have a better role model than that? I devoured all other car and motorcycle titles I could afford to buy. But how was I going to achieve this dream of getting into journalism, let alone anything to do with racing cars or bikes?

The time had come to leave school and Mum, through her contacts, knew Mr Eric Bull, a reporter on our local weekly newspaper, *The County Express*. She wasn't keen on my becoming a journalist, with all the stories of reporters and the drinking ethic, and, of course, being the always sensible lady, she was right to worry and be concerned.

I think she got Mr Bull to our house to try to put me off, really, but it didn't. He was a mature, nice-suited, very level-headed man, and was at the top of his profession, as it were, on a local paper. You need to work hard and be keen to learn, I think he said; well, I could do that.

In life, sometimes you need a bit of luck, as well as skills and motivation. I wrote a letter to the owner of *The County Express*, Lt. Col. Moody, asking for a job as a trainee reporter and received a handwritten letter back, explain that there were no vacancies at that time and to try other local papers. He was an awe-inspiring man to me as well – over six feet tall and wore an intimidating flowing black cape when he ventured down Stourbridge High Street.

Most youngsters have to go out of their locality to find jobs, especially on newspapers. That was how it was done in those days in the 1960s; you were apprenticed to the paper and learnt the profession in-house, as it were, with day release courses to tune your journalistic skills. Not now when the first and only thing to do is get a place at university and get a journalism degree before you get a placement on a newspaper.

I believe the way I learnt was better, more constructive, more complete, but you can't stop progress and, for me, it was a godsend as I hadn't any qualifications to get a place at university. So, today, I might not even have had the chance. Luckily for me, I wrote again later and Lt. Col. Moody said they did have a position open for a trainee journalist and, this time, I was given the job. Well, not exactly. Moody handwrote a letter on *County Express* and *Dudley Mercury* headed notepaper saying: "We can offer you a job on the editorial staff and I suggest you try it out for a month or six weeks. At the end of that time, if you are suitable, you will be apprenticed in the normal way. Perhaps you will let me know the date on which you can start. Yours faithfully." The date was 26.8.63. I still have that letter in my files.

# CHAPTER ELEVEN

# Make the Tea, Edwards!

My new career had started. It was high-pressure stuff, making all that tea day after day for all those experienced reporters in our little smoke-filled room in Victoria Passage, just off the High Street, Stourbridge. I was under the pupillage of the chief reporter, Jack Haden, almost a Mr Pastry-looking character, with grey receding hair, and bottle glasses, always in a suit that had at one time been new, with trousers tucked into his socks when he went on his reporting rounds in the district on his ancient upright black bicycle, possibly a Raleigh, wearing a not-so-stylish black beret.

Mr Haden was one of the most well-known and respected people in the whole of Stourbridge and its environs. Not only was he the top journalist on the staff of *The County Express*, which was considered a "bible" for the whole of the community, where every birth, and death and everything in between, was reported, almost word for word as it happened. It was the internet and Facebook of its day. Everyone read the *County*, which came out weekly as a huge broadsheet newspaper – remember them? And you were in big trouble if you ever spelt anyone's name wrong, believe me.

But not only was Mr Haden the oldest and most respected journalist in the office, he was also a local historian, the most well-known of his day and wrote many learned books on the history of the town and places nearby, including tomes on the glass industry. His local knowledge was immense.

After what seemed like months of making the tea, I had other duties as well. One of the most turgid was, as soon as the week's paper had come out, I had to update the musty old files, for use in obituaries. With a sharp pair of scissors, I had to cut out any story in the massive paper, which, for instance, mentioned the mayor, Alderman X, or any authority figure of the day, etc., and date and place the cutting into a brown envelope to go with all the other cuttings which had been previously written about the person. These were used when they died and it was easier to compile an obituary on them from these files. It took forever and I hated it after a while. Some of the files on people were bulging and I did find it fascinating, reading of well-known local figures in public life from decades ago.

But I knew I was learning, things were sinking in about how a newspaper worked, how journalists went about finding stories, how to write them up, against deadlines. I was taught how important diary jobs were, i.e. council meetings and similar, and the off-diary stories, which were the best, as they had to come out of your own head, your brain, your intelligence, your knowledge. It was a challenge I was up for.

It was a pleasure to get out of the office and actually do a job. These could be visiting a golden wedding couple or a diamond wedding pair in their home, as they celebrated their years of wedlock. At least someone else made me a cup of tea that day. Getting old folks, who had led blameless and happy lives but had done nothing newsworthy, bless 'em, in 50 or 60 years, to say something that was at least interesting to our readers was incredibly difficult, sometimes an art which taxed me greatly!

Back in the office came another chore; wedding reports. I, as the newest, wet behind the ears, reporter was handed all these wedding reports which had taken place that week and sent in to the paper. The families of the brides were all given standard wedding forms to fill in for the paper – where the wedding took place, what the bride wore, often in great detail for this was of great importance to everyone apparently, where they were going on their honeymoon, what the bridesmaids wore, where they were going to live, on and on went the form. I had to "top and tail" the reports before they went in the paper. This meant picking out some feature from the handwritten report and making it the introduction, or "intro", into the piece. You had to be careful, though, as quite often all the wedding reports in one week were all very similar to each other and that was frowned upon. So, a simple task like this one was difficult as you could be pulled up and told to have another go.

It was so tedious and boring for a 16–17-year-old. Nothing like the reporters in books and on TV, who wore trilby hats pulled down over their faces, lurking up dark alleys, waiting for a story. But I was still learning and I was eager to do better.

I was found to be "suitable", as our caped commander had said in his letter to me, and my career continued after the trial period.

I had to learn about how to be a "real" reporter by attending a one-day release course for two years in Birmingham – the big city, as far as I was concerned. It held too many pleasures for me unfortunately, and I would have learned more about politics, current affairs, shorthand abilities, if I hadn't skived off too many times in the afternoons to see the latest Brigitte Bardot or Sophie Loren movie playing in "Brummagem"! But learn I did, and the necessary passes were obtained from the Institute of Journalists courses, thank goodness.

Gradually, it all began to make more sense to me and, with a greater confidence, I attended the smaller council meetings, then the larger authority ones and learned how to report on them properly without making mistakes.

I probably got more stories from the pub than from council meetings. A lesson for any aspiring journalist; it's often better to go "off-diary" for a story than rely on diary jobs like councils. That's what makes newspapers such glorious affairs, finding out about what's really going on in your community and writing them up for your readers. Which meant sometimes taking our alderman for a pint or two after the meeting and get him talking after the wheels had been oiled, as it were. Much better stories, and exclusive to you, as he'd not said it in a public meeting. That way you got to know what was really going on behind the scenes, not, maybe, for instant publication, but for future reference about many matters which were to make headlines later.

I learnt you need to get people's trust and respect and being local journalists that was important. Not to make too much of a prat of yourself comes in handy. And not to become a prima donna, as that was a big pitfall for some young whippersnappers still wet behind the ears. You didn't make the news; others did, and you had to report it. Not the other way round.

# CHAPTER TWELVE

# My Colleagues

Other names in the reporters' room were Alan Worrall, a bearded Lambretta owner who played trumpet in a trad band at the time, just before the Beatles changed everything. We got on well and I went to lots of gigs he did in the area. He was pretty good. I always liked my music, especially live, and Alan told me, whatever anyone else said, the band always played better when fresh and alert at the beginning of the show, and completely sober; they only sounded better to the paying public after the audience had had a pint or two. But after the band had had a pint or two, the music suffered! That's what he said.

Derek Elwell quite often wrote the opinion column in the *County*, which at the time I was envious of, as I had not the experience of the world that he had to write columns of his own, giving his own views, not of someone else. From him I learned much. His pet subject was that of the controversial adding of fluoride to our water. He was an expert on that. Boy oh boy, he wrote many opinions on that!

It took me a long time to realise he listened to you in a conversation and whatever you said, he would disagree with, to get a friendly argument going; he loved it. I sussed him out, eventually, but I was very naive before it clicked what he was doing. Lesson learnt. Then I tried to turn the tables on him, sometimes successfully.

He too taught me how to do a "running" story at a football match, when copy had to be sent over the telephone to a waiting copy-taker, before quickly summing up the match and getting the result correct, for the local "pink un"; the Saturday sports paper.

Steve – can't remember his second name – was a young blood who enjoyed a little snifter before getting into work in an early morning pub on the way into the office. I enjoyed his company and often on early, skiving days we would go off playing snooker or tenpin bowling. We got quite good because of the time we gave to following our sporting pursuits, with me playing what I thought was a smart, teenage role, smoking Peter Stuyvesant, the mildest cigarettes at the time. I think he smoked French Gauloises cigarettes in the office and they stank.

Unfortunately, I did get the pipe-smoking habit later on, through my father who smoked one, but never cigarettes like he did. Then, much later, the odd cigar with a pint but saw the folly and at last gave up the weed decades ago.

Mr Bowling, I believe, was our Halesowen district reporter, so I didn't see too much of him. My memory is of him puffing away with his cigarette never leaving his mouth as he bashed the keys of the typewriter like a navvy, filling the typewriter keys with ash from his ciggies. To use the typewriter after him you first had to shake it upside down to get rid of all the ash which had fallen inside the keys.

Then I was transferred from head office in Stourbridge to our Brierley Hill district office, which was really senior reporter, Phil Malpass, and a lady who manned the Albion Street front office taking ads, etc.

My apprenticeship continued with Phil, who taught me the ropes of my new manor, a more industrialised, working-class town than that of staid Stourbridge. It had the massive Round Oak Steel Works still in pungent operation and Marsh and Baxter; butchers with their factory and slaughterhouse in town. I swear, we once did a story where a pig escaped and ran riot in the High Street and ended up in a china shop; not a bull this time!

Phil was not your ordinary kind of journalist; he had been the captain and track record holder of Cradley Heath's speedway team down the road at Dudley Wood Stadium, in the 1940s and early 50s and helped the club revive in 1960, when I had started to go and follow the sport each Saturday night.

Phil rode professionally for the club for years but always remained a full-time reporter for the *County Express*, which was unique in the sport. He took his holiday weeks as days off to get to the team's away fixtures each season. For me, I was as happy as a sandboy; l listened avidly to all the tales of the club's early days from Phil.

He had retired before I started going, but I did see him have a one-off ride in the early 60s in a demonstration on his own round the famous Cradley track. No leathers for Phil, he simply rode a few laps in his lounge suit and tore the sole of his left shoe off as he put it on the ground to slide round the bends at relatively high speed. Amazing, but crazy. No crash helmet, either. Never be allowed now. Health and safety regulations, you know.

Regular work was gained from the Brierley Hill magistrates' court, conveniently next to the town's police station and opposite Warwick's pub, which was the office local. It was and is officially called The Three Crowns, but to us it was always "Warwick's" after the landlord, who always ran it very well. I remember his sister who must have been a very good classical pianist. Her practising used to echo down the stairs sometimes, very good it seemed to me at the time, but I never actually saw her play face to face, as it were, as I can recall.

The proximity to the magistrates' court was vital to some of Warwick's regulars. If they were due in court and expected to go down for a few months, they would drop into his pub for a couple of swift pints, before accepting their fate across the road in front of the local bench. Court work was demanding on your concentration as you had to have the facts completely correct and the spelling of all names spot on.

There was only once I was offered a bribe, outside the court, if I'd keep the chap's name out of the *County Express*. It didn't work. I held my ground. Magistrates' courts take the minor cases, like drunk and disorderly, riding a bike without lights, the odd bit of pilfering, that sort of thing, but there were some tougher criminal cases which had to be reported on. Most of them went up to the higher courts, who had tougher sentences they could impose on the defendants. It was an eye-opener for a while for me as a boy just out of his teens.

The Brierly Hill pub was working-class and all sorts of interesting characters used to drift through. But the one fact I remember about Warwick's was the colour of the bar's ceiling. It was a lovely sort of brownish colour, unique, nothing you'd see on the top of a paint tin colour chart. Bit of a light, kind of chocolate hue, with quite a nice shine to it. I asked why it was that particular colour and was told, many, many years ago it had been white and as it had never been painted, it was the colour the white had gone, due to the heavy smoking habit of the regulars, when smoking was allowed indoors, in pubs. The ceiling was the colour of nicotine, and I presume much the same colour as the lungs of the smokers themselves.

Warwick's was our lunchtime watering hole for years, where we'd meet up with many Brierley Hill characters, including the pig factory's foreman of the abattoir who had one less finger than most of us, having lost it in an argument with a pig he'd once got a bit too close to.

We quite often saw Alderman Tom Wells, a Labour man through and through, who I think must have worked at the steel works. We saw him after his shifts and after a pint or two of "mixed" – that is half a pint of Midlands bitter beer and mild beer, mixed together in a pint glass – he could be relied on to tell us some of the goings on behind the big stories about to break in the town. He was well connected to do this, as he was the mayor! It pays as a journalist to know the right people socially.

After a shandy or two, I'd be off to get my own cooked lunch back at my mum and dad's, only a few minutes' drive or ride back to Vicarage Road, then back to the office for the afternoon shift.

There was a daily round of checking with the local police to ask if anything had come in to their attention overnight which they could tell us about. Calls which were mighty important if you wanted to keep abreast of what was going on in your area. But quite tedious.

Reporting was, most of the time, regular calls, regularly done, because if you missed keeping in touch, nine times out of ten something big had happened which you *did* want to know about. It was still my duty to go round all the local churches and chapels to talk to the local vicars and pick up their parish magazines as soon as they came out, because some vicars made good copy with some of the comments they made in their mags. They loved the headlines they made in the paper! Still the golden and diamond weddings, of course; all the glamorous jobs! But it was, in the end, a great learning curve for the rest of my journalistic life.

There were turgid, to me, flower and vegetable shows to cover as well, and you had to get *all* of the results of each category as they all went into the *County Express*, woe betide you if you missed somebody's name who'd won best carrots or best broccoli.

And funerals, they could be a pain too. The *County* did funerals in full – that is, for the "important" public figures of our town. That included a full list of mourners and there could be hundreds of them in the church for the memorial service. My job was often to collect all these names, written in my reporter's notebook for turgidly typing out at the end of the funeral report in the office later.

At one big funeral, which I was covering alone, I arrived late, very late; all the mourners were already in the church as I arrived. I was in all sorts of trouble. It was a sizeable funeral with many, many mourners. As they started to pour out from the back doors, I somehow corralled them in with my arms outstretch, saying 'I'm from the *County Express*, can you give me your names please before you go?' It worked a treat and I got all of their names and I got away with it; never mentioning it to anyone back at the office. It did help that, in those days, people wanted to get their names in the local paper, and being a mourner was one time they were happy to have their name in print.

There was a one big plus point about funerals, though. We had a request from the evening paper boys to cover a funeral of note for them, as they didn't want to waste their time and efforts in attending. So, us weekly newspaper reporters were tasked to do a report including a list of mourners for them, fairly reasonably openly,

I believe, despite the fact we worked for another newspaper. It was all paid for by the evening paper as "linage". That is, the stories were paid for by the line, so the more mourners, the more money for us. It was a great source of extra beer money. This supplemented our weekly wage, which was in cash stuffed in a small brown envelope. Pound notes, ten-shilling notes and coins.

# CHAPTER THIRTEEN

# Rule Number One – Don't Get Scooped!

A t the Brierley Hill district office, away from the gaze of Mr Haden, Phil was his own boss, now helped by his new boy, me. I learnt how to play the game, work hard when you had to, always attend all diary jobs promptly, look for extra off-diary jobs all the time, but, most importantly, each day, at around 3pm, get hold of a copy of the evening paper's early edition, which was easy as it was in the same street as our office, to check if we had been "scooped" by them.

If there was a story we'd missed, we had to have a quick phone round to get the story ourselves, or do a quick rewrite, if not too important, before typing up the story which had eluded us, put it in with other daily copy we had into a brown envelope before sending it to head office in Stourbridge.

This was my job. Decades before emails, and the internet, these specially printed newspaper bus parcels had to be physically put on a Midland Red bus by me, running up the road to catch the first bus available, and handing the item to the bus conductor or conductress for collection at the terminus in Stourbridge by other colleagues.

After we'd provided enough copy for that day between us and not been "scooped", I would be free to perhaps have a regular game of snooker with Steve, if he had finished his jobs, or go a bit further afield to the tenpin bowling alley towards Birmingham, or get my kit ready for an evening of badminton at the Stourbridge Institute club.

There were evening jobs to go to, but not too many to be uncomfortable. On really quiet news days, Phil used to drive me in his blue Ford Corsair to Bridgnorth, a few miles away, for lunch, usually on a farmers' market day, when High Town was packed with tractors outside the pubs, which were open all day. That was after dropping in to the Cider House at Quatt, for a treat of a half pint of home-brewed pear cider, lovely on a warm summer's day.

There were serious news stories to cover; fatal road accidents, tragic house fires, etc. We never chased any ambulances or police cars. Tragic events had to be covered in any community, however. Most of the work Phil used to do seemed to be covering Brierley Hill's municipal council. Reports were long, councillors remained on their feet for ages, while Phil took down all their statements, knowing they were making the *County* pages.

But Phil had a unique way to shut up councillors and, indeed, have a meeting called to an end. If he'd had enough of the interminable political debates, perhaps as closing time was fast approaching, he'd noisily shut his notebook, close it, slam it onto the desk, on which he then put his feet. As the councillors knew they would not get speeches into the paper, they sat down. Worked every time. Brilliant. And it's all true. I was there.

I once had a D notice served on me. D notices were an agreement between government and newspapers not to report stories which might impinge on national security! Like maybe mentioning the whereabouts of an underground seat of government, to be used, for instance, if nuclear bombs were dropped on us, during the Cold War and the Cuban Missile Crisis – that sort of thing.

I do not recall the story I was working on, but it obviously touched a nerve when I tried to get a quote from a government department. I was just told by the editor that the story had been "spiked", meaning it was not going in the paper, as the *County Express* would not have gone against such strong-armed tactics from governmental agencies of the time, nor would anyone at that time, other than fearless, crusading journalist, Chapman Pincher, in the *Daily Express*!

Decades later, I found out about the existence of the Drakelow Tunnels and their secret. There's about three miles of them, some 18-foot wide and 16-foot high, near Wolverley, Kinver. Rover used the underground factory during the war, making engines for the Bristol Aeroplane Company.

In the 1950s, Drakelow had another use, that of a regional seat of government and was improved for some

30 years, including apparently new blast doors. Underground seats of government were for use in the Cold War in the '50s and '60s, for if Russia had dropped their atomic bombs on us as we bombed them. They were intended somehow for the country to try to fix itself after such a catastrophe, which had shattered Japan with the bombing of Hiroshima and Nagasaki. For our government to still take charge and rebuild. That was the plan anyway.

The government decommissioned the tunnels in the 1990s and the land was sold. I reckon, I had inadvertently made a reference to this secret, hence the D notice. Who knows, it might have been some other secret government facility we had in our circulations area, but I reckon it was this place! There are many of these once secret underground places of command in the country and the thought of them is very chilling, to think of what they were planned for, after millions of people had died horrific deaths from nuclear bombs, the fallout and the devastation they would have left.

On a lighter note, I do seem to have a knack while reporting in public places to be near people who lose body parts! Don't worry, it's not that gruesome. At an inquest, in Dudley, I remember a reporter from a rival paper next to me scrabbling across the table with his hand to retrieve his glass eye, which was merrily bouncing across the desk. Very embarrassing for him.

Many years later, I was covering a case in Northampton's Crown Court when a barrister lost a tooth on the front bench and a halt was called for repairs. The court was emptied of the jury and public, but I, as a court logger who worked for the courts, remained with other staff after he bought a tube of super glue and he fixed the tooth or denture back in place, while remaining at the front bench. The judge, jury and public were recalled and the trial continued.

# CHAPTER FOURTEEN

# Brother Dave's Story

M y brother now tells us his story:

I was born in late 1938, to Stanley and Mary, just in time for WWII.

Early memories are unreliable, of course. The family dog, Rusty, jumped out of an upstairs window to get to some noisy kennels up the road, but he eventually had to be put down when I started to take over his territory, which he resented. I have that on my conscience.

I think I used to be transported around our substantial garden in a wheelbarrow by Dad but that may have been an idea from an old photo I have seen, it may have been my second cousin, Bobby, who was being pushed around by his dad, Ken Phillips?

I remember vividly being left to walk to the Enville Street infants' school from Amblecote Church on my own, after a few trial runs with Mum. I finally plucked up courage to do this, clutching my Mickey Mouse gas mask and sandwiches for lunch.

My brother Dave at 13, in the back garden at Amblecote on his lightweight bike from Dad, which came to a sad end!

I was very finicky about what I ate, especially vegetables, which was not a plus, especially during wartime. I was given special dispensation to lunch with Mum's cousin, Albert, and his wife, Vera, who lived just across from the school, which spared me from the horrendous school dinners, although I did drink the school milk.

I also remember shopping with Mum at, for example, the Stourbridge Co-op butchers in Market Street, using our precious allowance of coupons from our ration books. I think that we used the Co-op in Brettell Lane, Amblecote, for other commodities. You had sections in the ration books for sugar, meat, fats, bacon and cheese.

Under the Lend-Lease system from the USA, the UK received aid of war material plus food (bread, flour, oatmeal, meat, potatoes, milk and eggs). From 1948, we received fantastic food parcels from Australia, often distributed via the school system. I remember having to swallow regular doses of cod liver oil.

A young Jack Dunford used to deliver milk direct from the farm up the road to the houses around using a motorcycle and sidecar which was used to carry a large milk churn.

During the war, Dad built an air raid shelter of sorts, made up of corrugated iron sheets. It was only partly buried in the ground, whereas next door had a really professional job which might have stood a chance of surviving a very indirect bomb blast. The only risk being bombs jettisoned at random by planes returning from raids on Birmingham.

On occasions we visited Doctor Greenbaum in the basement practice in the north side of Enville Street. Mum was criticised for using a Jewish doctor but she would not be influenced by that. I also remember shopping with Dad at the hardware store on the east side of Lower High Street and being fascinated by the overhead pneumatic system which was used to transport the cash and accounts.

To celebrate Victory Europe (VE) Day, a large bonfire was lit, which was placed in the middle of the road, not far from the house, but we were very aware that we still had to defeat Japan.

When sugar rationing finished in 1948, I bought Mum some chocolate from Miss Breeze's shop nearly opposite our house, thus earning welcome brownie points. You could also buy a bag of broken biscuits for a penny, I think.

From the infants' school, I moved to Enville Street Primary School and I remember the terrifying first day when all of us new kids were stood up against the wall by the bigger inmates! I was not a good student and was surprised one day to be given a sealed envelope from the headmaster to take home to Mum. He had quite given up on me and was surprised when I passed the eleven-plus for entry to the King Edward VI Grammar School in Stourbridge. This was the height of my academic career for a very long while. I slid downhill for a very long while, from 1A (under Daisy Druller, English literature and Latin) to 2B, 3C, 4G (G for general) where I at last started to wake up, scraping into the second science stream (5S2) to finish off apart from a few weeks in 6C (for commercial), where we were supposed to be learning shorthand and typing with the headmaster's secretary, Miss Bunn (no jokes please). The only other student, Malcom Wright, who I still keep in touch with, went onto qualify as an accountant. (I too later ended up in 6C – Andrew).

In the 1940s we would receive occasional home visits from our (older) second cousin, Jack Lloyd, who was at the grammar school. Whereas it was nice to catch up with him, we dreaded his visits because he would eat all our goodies, homemade treacle tart and shortcake, for example, if we were not careful. He was quite a big lad. We would visit their house in Brierley Hill occasionally. Jack Sr was a big bloke, and he was a bell ringer at the local church.

I could have received a fantastic education if I had applied myself, instead of being an idiot who was always thinking of what prank I could get up to next. There were some real characters amongst the staff. "Chalky" White was of quite small stature and had a withered arm and one day, a boy who was causing trouble was dealt with in a way which earned him great admiration. Mr White quietly strolled to the back of the room and lifted the boy out of his seat by the scruff of his collar and carried him to the front of the class and deposited him in the waste bin! (I later played badminton with Mr White at the Stourbridge Insititute – Andrew).

Other characters were "Bodger" Timbrell (who had been an industrial chemist) who regaled us with stories, like "there I was, standing with nitric acid dripping down my back", and Mr Spry, who made up his own concoctions for treating his stomach ulcer on a Bunsen burner. When he was out of the room, we would switch on our Bunsen burners and blow the gas down the reticulated system so that his burner went out. He used to get the gas company in to explain the problem and he never twigged what was going on.

The headmaster's name was Chambers (and while I was at the school too – Andrew). Shortly after I arrived at the school, the sixth formers, who were due to leave, painted "Up the Pot" on the High Street roofline of the façade; an act which made the local paper, of course. Later on, he gave me "six of the best" for taking a crow scarer to school (which was a stupid thing to do). That sobered me up a bit – no hard feelings.

CHAPTER FIFTEEN

# Dave the Farm Worker

When I was not at school, I spent lots of time working on the Amblecote Hall Farm, just up the road from us, on the other side of the railway bridge. Jack Dunford Jr ran the farm as his dad had retired by then.

Occasionally, for a few summer weeks, gypsies would camp just at the end of the farm drive, with their caravan and horses. A young lad about my age would do some manual work with me to earn a few bob, like hoeing, for example.

The farm was an interesting mix of arable and dairy with the complication that there was quite a lot of mining for coal going on underground, with a walk down pit not far away and the odd mine shaft. There were many "crownings in", with holes appearing unexpectedly with the pit props being exposed.

On one occasion, Jack Jr did not appear for his evening meal as usual and his dad went looking for him. He found him perched gingerly on top of the Nuffield tractor which was precariously balanced on the edge of a hole which had opened up. He was too scared to move. His dad coaxed him down and they managed to retrieve the situation later, but I cannot remember how.

Apart from doing manual work on the farm, hoeing and harvesting, etc., I was allowed to drive the David Brown tractor with which I carried out mowing, ploughing and harrowing operations. It was great fun.

The area of interest (for me anyway) was taken up mainly by the Withymoor Village estate, which is bounded roughly by the railway to the west, the canal to the north and Vicarage Road in the south-east. In the fifties, it was a fascinating industrial/agricultural mix. The railway line had a fire continually burning in its embankment with work being done on Sundays to try to rectify this. The canal had industrial firms along its banks, for example chain-making factories, with the chains being used for some of the big ocean liners of the day.

The farm was situated mainly in the south and east of the area on either side of Vicarage Road, and extending in the Stourbridge direction, before they commenced building houses there. The area in the middle was mainly taken up with the clay operations – miniature railway lines and trucks, with the brick-making factory to the south-east of Vicarage Road. The so called "brickle-wenches" were a tough bunch of female workers who mainly lived locally. Apparently, our nanna, Grandad Edward's wife, worked there at some stage. There were some tennis courts nearby, which Mum and Dad joined shortly after they were married.

Every Sunday, in the late '50s, we would visit our Aunty Kathleen in Wollaston, walking from our house in Amblecote, irrespective of weather and initially pushing brother Andrew in a pram. Aunty was a kindly but liberated woman who was assistant matron at a Birmingham Hospital. She had all her ribs removed down one side when she underwent lung surgery for TB. She never complained and loved doing puzzles and made the most delicious cheese pasties.

The Poole family lived in a house next to the farm. Basil Poole was a mining engineer and I was very friendly with his son, Jonathan. They had two daughters also, Anne (the eldest of the family) and Judith, the youngest. Anne studied agricultural engineering and later married Jack Dunford.

Jon was very mechanically minded. For example, we bought a 1932 Austin 7, which we almost completely refurbished, stripping the engine down completely and rebuilding it, from which we learnt a lot. The differential had a whine and it was the only part that we did not fix. We cheekily wrote to British Leyland for advice and they sent us details of how to do the work but it needed special tools to do this which we did not have.

We managed a trip in the Austin to the Lake District, travelling up the newly opened M6 at a flat out 40mph. Unfortunately, after a few days of hillwalking, the car was, ominously, only driving on one wheel and the half-shaft gave out halfway between Kendal and Keswick. You have to replace the half shaft from inside the differential housing and we did not have the tools to do that, but a friendly lorry driver, travelling north, lent us his tools with the promise that we would leave them the other side of the drystone wall so that he could pick them up on his return journey. We borrowed a few stones from the nearby wall to jack the car up and Jon hitchhiked to pick up a new half shaft (the same as a Morris 8 half shaft, we found.) Problem solved, thanks to the kindness of the lorry driver.

We would walk and cycle everywhere, including the canal towpaths, and out to the hills at Kinver and Clent.

I was a member of the Amblecote Scouts for a few years where I learnt some useful skills; camping and knot-tying, for example. One memorable scout camp I remember was at Dawlish in Devon, where we pitched our tent on top of a hill facing the sea. There was a huge storm one night with the wind screaming in from the direction of the sea, accelerating as it came up the slope.

This happened in the middle of the night and our tent was the first to go since it was weakened by the fact that "Ocker" Bray had been swinging on the ridgepole earlier in the day and broken it in half. Most of us gathered in the marquee trying to keep it upright by hanging on to the central pole, which we succeeded in doing. Next day we found items of clothing scattered all over the field and much wider. Fortunately, I had had the sense (unusual for me) to put all my clothes into a bag earlier.

Time came to find a job. There was plenty of work around in those days (late '50s) it seemed, but I had no idea what I wanted to do. An accountant over the road (Mr Growcot) found me a job with Lloyds Bank as a clerk, which I was not very enthusiastic about but decided to give it a try.

My first job was with their Netherton branch, right in the heart of the Black Country. I posted ledgers by hand and not much else as I was a "supernumerary". My only claim to fame was when I left my half of the bank vault keys at home and had to ask Mother to bring them in on the bus which she kindly did. Netherton had one of the most famous public houses in the Black Country, which was called the Old Swan Inn, but was better known as Ma Pardoe's.

Then it was off to the bank training college at Hazelhurst, Surrey, which was a disaster as I had no interest in the proceedings, struggling to understand that debits and credits were different, depending on which side of the counter you stood. I was warned I was close to getting the boot and that I must lift my game.

Lloyds Bank, Edgbaston, Birmingham was my next posting, still as a "supernumerary". Major Hobson was the manager and a nice bloke but you did not see much of him except in the gents' toilets when I was late and frantically trying to change out of my sweaty cycling clothes (I often cycled in from Stourbridge; a distance of about 12 miles). Hobson seemed pretty relaxed about this but the accountant hated me – perhaps he hated all juniors. Tiny (he was well over six feet tall) ran the branch with terrifying efficiency and authority. If you wanted time off for something you had to catch him early in the day because he became more and more belligerent as the day went on, which had something to do with his visits to a public house nearby during the day. If you crept out of work for a bit, you always seemed to meet him coming the other way on the zebra crossing, which did not improve his temper. The job was made just tolerable by the pleasant staff and particularly the office girls! One of the stupid things that I could not understand was why we had to stay behind sometimes if the day's work did not balance by as little as a penny. They would not let you put a penny in the till (or take one out) which I found most frustrating and stupid.

We used to get these terrible fogs (or, rather, smogs) in those days from the industrial pollution and coal fires in many houses. On one particular day, the smog was so bad that the Midland Red buses stopped running and I missed the last one going home to Stourbridge.

Fortunately, the town buses were still running so I managed to get a lift out to the town boundary. I started to jog towards home and as I as descending Mucklow Hill, I heard the noise of what sounded like a bus through the fog. Then a bus loomed out of the gloom and I managed to jump on the open platform of the last Midland Red bus to Stourbridge. I have told this story many times and nobody believes me, but it is true!

# CHAPTER SIXTEEN

# Dave's Royal Navy Days: Bliss

I was just waiting to start my two-year national service. The momentous day arrived and I strolled down to the armed services recruitment centre in Broad Street, Birmingham, with much trepidation. I was met by a very pleasant officer in a uniform I did not recognise. He asked which service I would prefer to serve in. I was taken aback by this because I did not think that I had much choice. The Royal Navy, I said, not thinking I had a chance as I had visions of standing guard duty in Germany somewhere in the freezing cold, where a lot of national servicemen ended up. He asked me to do a simple test to show that I was not completely stupid and said that I was in. Later, I realised that the recruiting officer was a master at arms in the Royal Navy (which was roughly equivalent to a regimental sergeant major). So, I had said exactly the right thing by accident and was recruited to be a telegraphist, training in Morse code, radio operating and code work.

National Service was, on the whole, a benefit to me because it gave me time to sort out what I wanted to do in life, despite a few low points (like the initial basic training!). What follows is nothing whatsoever to do with the Black Country but it may be of some interest now that National Service is long gone.

Shortly after arriving at HMS *Raleigh* (Devonport) I remember initially looking across the Tamar River into Cornwall and wondering what was to come. This was soon relieved when another 13 chaps started to turn up from all corners of the UK to form the class of "Watkins Telegraphists". They were a great bunch of youngsters and we never had a serious argument during the entire time that we were together. It was February 1958.

We were posted to Saint Budeaux (an old prison camp overlooking part of the docks area), which was shared, but strictly segregated from, a WRNS unit next door. We were in skills training for the best part of a year. Our instructor was a petty officer telegraphist (special), or POTS for short, a usually amiable bloke who we greatly respected. He had been sunk twice during WW2. On the odd occasions when we played up, POTS had an unusual way of dealing with us. We would be sent off to get our gas masks and made to put these on. He then marched us up and down the slippery slopes of the camp, with us initially slipping and sliding in our hob-nailed boots. He would then stop us and say that every time one of us slipped from that time on we would do it again for as long as was necessary. We got the message.

In February 1959, we all got posted to Malta in the Mediterranean, to join 104 and 108 Squadrons of 360-ton, double-mahogany-hulled, coastal class minesweepers named after UK villages. The 14 of us were dispersed between the two squadrons of 16 ships total, so that everywhere you went in the Mediterranean you almost always met up with at least one of your mates. My boat was the *Wilkieston*, which was the junior (canteen) boat in 104 Squadron. Our main task was to try to stop arms smuggling into Cyprus in six-week patrols, with several minesweepers being used, together with a supporting frigate, to cover designated areas off the Cyprus coast. We patrolled mainly at night, often with our navigation lights off and our radar on, without much success, it seems, apart from incidents like rescuing caïques (local fishing boats) full of drunks who got lost on their way across the narrow straight from the mainland. Perhaps they were the arms smugglers? Or maybe they crossed over during the day when we were not looking?

If we were not in Famagusta (our base), we were on patrol in our designated area and the crew not on watch would go ashore in the ship's boat for a swim off the beach during the day. Even the duty watch were allowed to swim around the anchored ship to typically play water polo with the ship's dog, a much-loved Labrador-cross which was recruited from the Battersea Dogs Home in Chatham after the commissioning of the ship in Chatham a few months previously.

There are so many stories about the ship's dog, the most famous being as follows. The two squadrons of minesweepers (16 ships in all) were lined up abreast, practising sweeping for magnetic mines, each pulling about 1000ft long electric cable. The seamen on the after deck of the *Wilkieston* were playing with the dog by throwing a beer can around for her to chase and catch when the beer can inadvertently went over the stern with the dog in pursuit. The lads promptly phoned the bridge to report what had happened. The captain threw down his hat and jumped on it before reporting to the senior squadron commander what had happened and asked permission to pick up the dog and this was fortunately granted. They wound in the cable and turned 180 degrees to try to find the dog, who was found, still swimming strongly, with the beer can still in its mouth.

Back in Malta, the sailors decided that it was only right that the dog should be allowed to experience motherhood. A kidnap party was despatched to scour the streets surrounding the Sliema Creek waterfront to find a suitable mate. Unfortunately, the only dog that they managed to grab was one half her size; a scrawny white mongrel. Back on board, any attempt at mating failed until the ship's carpenter constructed a small table for the dog to stand on. Success at last. Later six puppies, which looked very much like their mum, were born in Singapore, with the progeny being distributed around some of the rest of the minesweepers. The litter was a bit of a handful early on, however, as the pups had to be rescued regularly as they were likely to fall in the water, especially before their eyes opened.

The Royal Navy no longer issues a rum ration as it did in my time in the service. Every day, usually as we waited in the queue for lunch, ratings would receive a tumbler of (then) over-proof Jamaican rum (the tot) in the ratio of two parts of water to one of rum. It certainly improved your appetite to compensate for the occasional ordinary meal and made you feel good. Petty officers received their rum undiluted. At sea, if the weather was rough, we would sometimes forego our tot and only the most hardened sailors (usually three-badge, or twelve-year sailors) would imbibe. I can remember the ship's cook and the leading hand sitting down in our mess playing cards, with a fanny (bucket) of rum between them!

When not in Cyprus or Malta, or in transit between the two, the *Wilkieston* managed a few visits to Taormina in Sicily, La Spezia in Italy, Tripoli, Haifa in Israel, and Beirut, which was then known as the "Paris of the Middle East". How things, sadly, have changed.

Later, in 1959, we heard that the two squadrons were to sail for Singapore; apparently this was something to do with troubles in Laos. National servicemen were to be returned to the UK as we were not supposed to travel east of the Suez Canal. One by one my mates disappeared, and I barely showed my face on deck, keeping my fingers crossed that I would be forgotten about, which I was. Passing through the Suez Canal, we were last in line, with an Egyptian gunboat right up our stern (it was not long after the Suez Canal debacle in 1956).

We stopped in Aden, Mumbai, Colombo (Sri Lanka) and finished up in dry dock in Singapore as it was our turn for a partial refit. I had my 21$^{st}$ birthday in Colombo, buying all the crew a drink (Tiger beer) and of course they all bought me one back. I did my best but the result was predictable. The rule on returning to your ship was that you were required to walk unaided up the ship's gangway. I failed the test badly but this was overlooked on this special occasion by the officer of the watch.

Life in Singapore (it was a very interesting place in those days!) was idyllic with nothing to do except swim in the pool and "go ashore". That was until they suddenly realised I needed to be sent back to the UK as my national service period was almost up. I did not want to return in winter (February) if I could help it, but it was either going back pronto or signing on for nine years. I decided to go back but managed some leave by travelling up through Malaysia (on a little Wild West-like rail journey up through the jungle) to Penang. I was soon recalled to Singapore and promptly flown back to Blighty on a 24-hour flight on a RAF Bristol Britannia. I arrived in Plymouth barracks just in time for final celebrations with all my mates.

It was great to get home again but, like too many servicemen, I suppose, I missed the comradeship of the group that I had been with for nearly two years, when you always have someone to talk to and to "go ashore" with. Most of my friends had moved on or got married and so on and you have to start again to make new friends. I was so incredibly lucky to have had such a great time during national service when so many others did not, especially those who were on active service.

# CHAPTER SEVENTEEN

# Dave Back in Blighty

The Withymoor Village Estate was well in progress when I returned, with many houses under construction. Apparently, they dug an enormous hole to get all the coal out, and the farm, fields, pits (clay and coal), mineral railway lines, etc., had all gone.

They rerouted Amblecote Road and widened it, of course. It is very strange that, although it was obvious this was all for the good, I missed the old farm and industrial landscape terribly. This was completely stupid, I know, but that is the Peter Pan in me, I suppose.

I moved to Hull to study for merchant navy radio officer qualifications, but quickly decided that I would not go back to sea and I started to study for more electronic technician qualifications, particularly after finding the radio officer Morse studies much beneath the level of skills that we had achieved in the Royal Navy. It was only a skill, but we had a real pride in what we did.

My brother Dave, me and Dad in Burwood, Vicarage Road, Amblecote after Mum had died. That door with white paper panels was always warped and never shut properly; part of the wonky house!

I would often hitchhike from Hull to Stourbridge at the weekends, doing this in one lift on one memorable occasion. But it was not as easy to get lifts as previously, when you were in uniform.

In 1961, Jon Poole and I drove down to Istanbul and back in one of the first Leyland Minis to come off the production line. Yugoslavia was one country then and we passed through Bulgaria, which at this time was behind the "Iron Curtain". The Mini caused quite a bit of interest. We flew across the English Channel both ways (from Lydd to Le Tourquet and return) with the Mini on board. Cars were driven in through the nose of the aircraft and passengers boarded in the normal way to their seats.

Moving back to the Midlands, I got a job in Bridgnorth, Shropshire, as a test radio technician with the company Automatic Telephone and Electric, continuing my studies at Wolverhampton Technical College and still living at home in Amblecote.

I spent a lot of time walking in North Wales and did a bit of caving in South Wales too. I have kept up with several of my walking mates from Bridgnorth over many years. At about that time, Andrew and I persuaded Dad to spend a weekend with us in Snowdonia. We booked in at the Hotel Gorphwysfa (now a YHA) on the top of the Llanberris Pass and we did part of the "Snowdon Horseshoe" route, including the PYG track and returning via the Snowdon summit and Crib Goch.

Dad went well – he must have been in his mid-50s, which we thought was old then! In those days, there was no running water upstairs in the hotel and in the bar; beer was dispensed via a large jug which was brought up from the cellar.

Mum's dad, our Grandad Hicks, lived with us at home. He worked in the Stourbridge glass industry at one of their Amblecote factories, largely making items such as wine glasses and bowls and many other glass items, which were often then cut. They produced some beautiful pieces. He always took a glass bottle of cold tea to drink with his lunch.

It was very hot working so close to the furnaces. When he retired, he would get up late and make his porridge, which he always ate from the saucepan, much to Mum's disgust. He would then visit the toilet where he would sit and read the *Daily Express* newspaper. A man of regular habits.

Every week he studiously filled in the football pools competition, but he never seemed to win anything, despite his considerable knowledge of the game. He had played the game in his youth with some success and he was an accomplished lawn bowls player, winning many medals. He "scouted", acting as a talent spotter for two football league teams on an honorary basis; Portsmouth and Hull City, I think.

Apart from the travel involved in that pursuit, he walked everywhere, rarely using a bus. Every evening, he would walk to the "Institute" at the Fish, in Amblecote and have a quiet beer before walking home. During the war, at weekends, he would sometimes walk to visit some

THE HOUSE THAT WOULDN'T FALL DOWN

associates at The Anchor Inn, Caunsall, near Kinver Edge, where I suspect he may have traded some pieces of glassware for pork meat, as there were pigs kept at the back of the pub. Many years later, Grandad asked me to take him to this pub by car, but nobody remembered him which was a bit disappointing, but predictable, I suppose.

To qualify as a chartered engineer, I had to go down to London (where I worked for Cossor Electronics in Harlow, Essex) so that I could study at the Northern Polytechnic (as it was then). After obtaining professional qualifications, I moved nearer to home, taking a job with Hartley Electromotives in Shrewsbury, walking in North Wales most weekends. I met a bunch of climbers there and we had some great times. Our Sunday night sessions, downstairs in the Mytton and Mermaid pub on the Shrewsbury bypass, became legendary amongst climbers.

And then (to reward myself for all those years of part-time study?), I did a three-year contract with the Zambia Police, training Zambian radio technicians. It was a waste of time career-wise but I would not have missed it for anything, doing a lot of travelling around, including many game reserves in Zambia, Tanzania, Kenya, Rhodesia and South Africa (before this became popular and before the poachers swung into action, sadly). It was mid-1971 when I returned to the UK, having got married to Christine, from Cheadle Hulme, who had been teaching at the local technical college in Lusaka.

After further study (at what is now Portsmouth University) and a very interesting few months with

Ferranti Microwave Division in Wythenshawe, Manchester, we moved to Australia in late 1972, with regular visits back to Blighty to see our parents while they were still alive. We have lived in Sydney, Perth, Tasmania and Queensland.

But still some of the best years were in the '50s and '60s, back in the old country.

## CHAPTER EIGHTEEN

# Dad's Story; A Sportsman all his Life

My dad, Stanley, was born on September 24, 1907, son of Richard and Maria Edwards, who lived in Pensnett and other houses, around six in all, in Oldswinford, and finally Wollaston, with his sister, Kathleen, who never married.

Richard, Dad's father, was a blacksmith, but we have no record of where this work was done. It is an accepted fact in the family – that is my brother and I – that Dad never talked much about his side of the family. The exact opposite of Mum, who wrote a book about hers! That's the way it was. Bless him.

Dad had five uncles and three aunts, who were his mother's siblings, and nine cousins – children of those aunts and uncles.

One right out of the archives! That's our Dad as a very young child at his house in Oak Street, Kingswinford. He was born in 1907.

Dad with his athletic build as a young man on the beach in a classy one-piece bathing costume! Powerful legs for cross country running, his life's passion.

Mum's caption on photo says: "1991, Bowling club members viewing Stan's handiwork re: cross country memories, from left, Stan, Roy Luther, Cyril Flavell, Jack and Bill Lees." The display case was just part of Dad's history of Stourbridge athletic clubs he put together for display at Stourbridge Library that year. A proud achievement.

We do know that Dad was very ill as a child, possibly lucky to survive. He had a bout of double pneumonia when tuberculosis was a killer disease and didn't go to school until he was seven years old. I believe he would have attended, probably for months, the Kinver Recovery Hospital, where fresh air was the decided route to combat the terror diseases. But survive he did and grew stronger to take part in a lifelong passion of athletics and was in at the beginning of organising clubs in the Stourbridge area.

His favourite pursuit was cross-country running. Running came first, while Mum, in their courting days, came second; that's Mum's memory anyway! It was his passion in life and somehow fits in with his personality. He was alone, in the countryside, battling the elements, physically and mentally, and it fitted him well; always keeping fit and trim throughout his long life. That is not to say he was a loner, far from it, he enjoyed people, always had a smile and joined in well, and was an entertaining conversationalist.

But he liked cross-country running too, where he could extend himself. He certainly liked the camaraderie of other competitors.

Athletics clubs in Stourbridge go back to 1926 with the founding of Stourbridge Birchfield Harriers and slightly later came the Stourbridge British Legion Athletic Club, and in 1929, a sports meeting was proposed at the Stourbridge War Memorial Ground, Amblecote, just opposite where our house was situated in Vicarage Road, Amblecote.

Dad's name first appears in the athletics history of the town in 1931 when he served as the club secretary with his friend, Joe Lees, his assistant secretary. The Lees' were a famous athletics family from Wordsley with ten brothers! Most were runners, but also footballers and swimmers.

Stourbridge British Legion AC came into being at the Seven Stars Hotel, Hagley Road, in the town, in 1928. The first club dinner was at the Bell Hotel, Market

Street, in the town on February 28, 1929; the cost was three shillings per head. The club was fortunate that the governors of King Edward VI Grammar School (headmaster at the time, Mr J E Boyt) agreed for them to use their Amblecote sports field for training. The groundsman, Harry Shotton, was paid three shillings per evening for the extra work and senior members paid one shilling and sixpence for the first season.

The grammar school field was in Vicarage Road, Amblecote, only a few hundred yards from our house; number 41. And my brother, Dave, and I were to use that ground for sports during our time at the school.

The club held their second annual British Legion (Stourbridge branch) Athletic and Cycling Sports meeting at the War Memorial Athletic Ground, at the bottom of Vicarage Road.

Affluent young people today would be astonished at the next information. Following the national general strike in 1926, financial recovery was slow and many members were still out of work. In 1928/29 the club purchased several pairs of running shoes from J P Davies, a Brierley Hill sports outfitter, and members purchased them with weekly payments. They had no money for outright purchases.

Winter training HQ in 1929 was the Cross Inn, Oldswinford. Club cross-country events in 1929/30 were held in Sutton-in-Ashfield, a youth's race, Edgbaston Reservoir, and a junior championship in Cwmbran, South Wales.

When equipment was needed, it was homemade. Twelve hurdles were made by Dick Ketteridge and transported to the grammar school ground by Mr Reading in his milk lorry. The club seemed to move around to a lot of pubs in the area and Mitchell & Butlers Ltd., the local brewery, said they were prepared for the club to use the Star & Garter pub, Norton as their winter HQ. The club kept that pub as its HQ until 1944, "not without some wartime hiccups" when presumably the pub had to shut, possibly not having any beer. That year, Tom Lees was elected captain and brother, Joe, trainer.

My brother, Dave, can remember visiting the Norton pub when he was young after Dad had been out competing in events. 'My dad and his mates used to wash in tin baths in the hotel courtyard after their runs,' he said.

The Wordsley family, name of Lees, was always associated with Stourbridge Harriers. There were 10 brothers in all and with the exception of Jim, who was a footballer and swimmer, they all won prizes as runners. Joe Lees introduced his brothers Tom, Jack and George to Stourbridge British Legion. Then came Harry, Edward and Bob.

It is good to note that the club had a ladies section at least from 1932 with Miss N Attwood as hon. sec! In 1933, the annual dinner was held locally in Amblecote, not in any Stourbridge pubs, on March 8 at Coxhill's Café, Upper High Street. That same year, four months later in July, the Stourbridge British Legion AC held its sixth yearly meeting at the War Memorial Ground,

Amblecote, which my father would have had a hand in organising and probably competing as well, but can't find his name among the winners of any classes!

The *County Express* did a page report on the mega event with two photos. It surpassed any of its predecessors, said the reporter, with field and track athletics events and cycling too and drew in a crowd of around 6000 people, so an important local event indeed for the area.

Dad's involvement with local athletics lasted his entire lifetime and obviously gave him much pleasure and enjoyment, being with other men following their passion for running, exercising for pleasure.

I, being born in 1945, have no recollection of the wartime shelter, built in the garden, but do remember Dad, my brother and I building a garage many years later with the same curved sheeting, adding iron girders between the two and a rough, flat roof, to make it a "double" garage, after Dad got his first car. I also do remember, as a child, looking down the menacing underground shelter in next door's garden, but I was never brave enough as a youngster to go down it!

Most of my memories of my Dad, are linked with memories of my mum and dad together with me. All our beautiful, wonderful holidays, paid for out of the holiday jar, trips to the Far Forest, cafes, days out, birthday treats, and, later, me taking them out on car rides when Dad had given up his driving licence, all inexplicably linked to "them" as a couple, a loving pair.

There were many more escapades, both at home and on holidays for us, all happy memories. A quiet man, but one who always liked a laugh. And a good night's sleep; late nights were not for him. He had a big heart and looked after my mum so well in her declining years, still coping, still having a laugh and a twinkle in the eye.

I got a smack once from him while very young on holiday on a beach. I kicked him between the legs from behind as he bent down. I *was* very young. I deserved a clout. Idiot.

Dave remembers Dad, who was in a reserved occupation during the war, had to swap jobs at the end of the conflict to make way for returning ex-servicemen. Luckily, he was not out of work for long, as Dave recalls, but it must have been a testing time for him and the family.

Another memory of Dad from Dave: 'I inherited his beautifully light bike which I modified and rode for years until I eventually destroyed it by riding off the steep end of the incredibly sloping old tennis court, caused by major subsidence, at Jonathan Poole's place. What a stupid thing to do, an act I strongly regret. I seem to remember the bike frame was made of 541 tubing which was incredibly light and possibly before its time.'

My sporting memories of Dad go back to when he used to regularly take me to see Stourbridge, walking down the road to the War Memorial ground, when I was a small boy. He taught me the rules of the game and I enjoyed my time watching the "Glassboys" with a cup of stewed, industrial strength tea from a large metal urn at half-time, while listening to the scores of the other games that day.

From early days, I can remember my first Stourbridge football hero, "Pagey", a right winger – Ernie, I think his name was – with thick, bow-legged, liniment-shined legs, as he sped down the touchline for a dramatic cross into the penalty area. That is my recollection, anyway, possibly with rose-tinted spectacles.

They always played in red and white striped shirts and because of the red colour and the fact I loved "Pagey", my first football shirt I asked for was an Arsenal shirt, number seven, of course. Red with long white sleeves, if I recall, with arms far too long for me!

If the ball was kicked out of play on one side of the pitch it disappeared down the "coal ole" into a factory yard, some 50 feet down, which, of course, was shut on Saturday, so a new ball was always on hand and I suppose the balls were retrieved by the club on a Monday morning from the firm!

A later hero of mine was Chic Bates, a very superior football player who went onto to play for higher league teams than Stourbridge and had a good managerial career too. A great goal scorer. Dramatic header.

I do have a clear memory of the great John Charles, the Welsh international, who, on his way back down the ranks of football, turned out for, I believe, Hereford, at Stourbridge. By then, much past his prime and a bit, shall we say, heavy, he was a bit of a clogger, bundling people over if they had the temerity to try to float past the old maestro half back as he had lost his speed. Still a fine header of a football even then, though.

Going over to our summer game, in the 1980s, Dad and I had a trip to London by train to see a match at the headquarters of cricket, Lords. It was, I think, all a revelation for Dad, travelling from Stourbridge Town station to London and picking up the London train, and thence to the London Underground, as he must have been pretty old by then. A trip he'd never made before.

We saw a county game between Middlesex and Northants and I think Dad remembered from that day the sight of Northants giant, Barbadian Vanburn Holder, in his pomp, bowling a cricket ball at very high velocity, not, perhaps, quite as menacing as his fellow West Indians at the time, Wes Hall and Charlie Griffith, but fast enough to intimidate many a batsman of that era! Great memories of my dad, taking it all in, in a most enjoyable day for both of us. I remember buying a Middlesex silk scarf for mum, which she wore for years, protecting her fragile neck.

We also had some trips to another glorious cricket ground, one of the finest county grounds in the country bar none; Worcester's Racecourse Ground. On one not so glorious day, a Sunday league game I think, the heavens opened and we sheltered under a tree for a while, until the electric storm overhead forced us and a lot of others into the Ladies Pavilion for glorious homemade cakes.

But for Dad, the ultimate sportsman, watching was not his best pleasure, playing was.

After his athletics career wound down, he was on the lookout for other sports to compete in and later on, he seriously took to golf, alongside many of his chums. Mum used to be embarrassed, when during his athletics career, which often took in a cross-country run, he took her to the cinema, but got cramp in his legs!

He had his own set of golf clubs for many years and played weekly for a long time on local municipal courses, never as a member of a club, I believe. On a couple of occasions, I accompanied him. To be honest, I wasn't very good and like many an amateur golfer, gave up eventually, saying golf is a good walk, spoilt. I could hit a glorious wood well down the fairway and then for the next hour or two would slice, jerk, top, all other balls into trees, undergrowth, with water hazards a particular favourite.

Once, I do remember, when playing with Dad, hitting a ball off the tee and striking a big tree just to the side of the green which then ricocheted the belligerent pill back to me, narrowly missing my head, as I skilfully and mercifully ducked. Enough was enough.

Tennis; yes, badminton; yes, golf; no. But Dad was stoically professional and he and his mates played until old age stopped them from turning out. Eventually 18 holes became nine, etc., but they kept going, like the old sporting troopers they were, to the end.

As golf ended, so bowls became the sport of choice. He and his cronies played the proper game of Black Country crown green bowls during the summer, and in the winter even got their own little club going to play indoor bowls, on mats. I know his great friend, Eric Nash, was involved as well. Where there was a way to play sport, they found it. Hats off to all of them.

When Dad was not playing sports, he was an avid gardener. He kept the reasonably sized lawn in the back garden trim with a push mower. Mum's favourite flowers, plants and trees were tended well and Mum enjoyed picking them, when her health allowed, for use in the house.

In their early days at Vicarage Road, Dad had a little friend. A dog called Rummy, I think, who would follow him all over the garden; whether he was digging, cutting, or whatever, the little chap was by his side, looking up with great devotion. He knew only one master and it was Dad. He was interested in no one else, not even Mum, I believe.

But when I was at home, we had a series of cats. Kimi and Mitzi were two names I remember and they were both well-loved family pets and had lovely, pampered lives as lucky cats do. One of our cats had toothache, and kept putting her paw over her mouth. Dad could see the problem tooth and got the poor thing between his knees in the living room and with a pair of pliers managed somehow with all the struggling – the cat, that is – to remove the sceptic molar. No vets bills for my dad.

As expected, the cat kept a fair distance from dad for a long while, with a look which said *don't you come near me*! But eventually he was forgiven!

As a boy, I kept mice, as you do, and I sold them to a local pet shop. Sixpence a time. Good money as I never did a paper round. They were nice, slow moving little pets, not like the outdoor variety of pests and we had them on our newspaper covered dining table sometimes. They liked specially to swing on the flowers. I think the cage was in the bathroom. The venture finished suddenly after one of the cats got through the open bathroom window and, as I had the mice in the empty bath to give them a little exercise out of their cage, ate them. I think Dad and Mum were quite glad, really.

When Mum became housebound, Dad did all he shopping. All the till girls at the local supermarket knew him by name and always helped him with his bag of groceries. He took up a posh plastic bag I'd given him – a present from a press trip to Monte Carlo – and he loved to tell the girls he'd just been there to see the Grand Prix! That was my dad, that was, great sense of humour.

Through keeping fit with daily walks, keeping himself busy and never having any more food than was necessary to keep himself going, he always had an upright stance, was lean with hardly an extra ounce of fat on him, had a full head of silver-grey hair, combed back, right to the end. He died aged 92 on November 12, 1999 at Wordsley Hospital, where his sister, our Aunty Kathleen, had been nursing in her day.

He lived alone for a couple of years after Mum died, still at the family home and looked forward to my weekend visits from Northamptonshire where I lived, always shaking my hand at the end of each visit as I got in the car to return home.

My brother, Dave, sums up our dad the best: 'In retrospect, Dad was a quiet, reserved bloke, always taking a back seat to Mum, who he adored. He was a good, caring father which we were so lucky to have.'

I visited him in hospital and brought him local history picture books to try to aid his failing memory, as his mind became confused. Poignantly, he thought his wife, Mary, our mum, was in the next ward. Bless him.

# CHAPTER NINETEEN

# Grandad's Story: The Black Country Glassmaker

My grandfather was William Richard Hicks, born on April 6, 1884 in Stourbridge.

Billy Hicks, as he was called, was a glassmaker all his life; a very skilled job which was obviously well paid. It should have been well paid, as the correct term for Stourbridge glass was lead crystal, meaning one of its major ingredients was lead, which gave off lethal fumes as it was used in the manufacture of the some of the best cut glass produced in the world.

But more of that historic Black Country industry will come later in Billy's story.

Grandad lived with my mum and dad at 41 Vicarage Road, his house, of course, which my parents moved into with him after their wedding in 1935. I grew up next to him, quite literally. He was a simple, man's man, who lived for his sport, never showing his emotion with regard to me or my brother, Dave. Work, jar or two in the pub or Amblecote Institute or the War

Memorial club, home for his dinner. Watching horse racing on TV, when we eventually had one, with the sound blaring out most afternoons, with Mum trying to keep calm, because there was nowhere else for her to go. There were only two rooms downstairs, and grandad had the downstairs "lounge" room as a bedsit.

And sport, he loved his sport. He was a local champion bowler, which was spoken as if the "ow" was is in "owl", so "bowler". Yes, you've got it. To him, it was never Birmingham either, it was always spoken of in the old style; Brummagem. And my mum was always "Mare" not Mary. He was always disappointed she was a girl. Never got over it.

I had a set of his bowls once but sadly let them go. He did give me a snooker cue which I used for decades, until it went missing from a snooker club in Desborough. I was gutted, it was a good cue.

Mum remembered seeing, in a shop window in town, a display of his recently won bowls trophies and medals, plus a handsome Kidderminster carpet, made just up the road in that famous weaving town. He was a bit of a sporting hero, liked the limelight and the attentions of his male friends.

Most clubs, pubs and institutes had their own teams and Mum happily went along with her dad and mum to watch the action.

Mum remembered, 'Mum and I sat on the lawns outside the greens for enjoyable hours watching the competitors and very good were these working-class men with the heavy bowls, making the bowl go right or left however they wanted, to follow the jack. Nearest the jack, won the "end". The Stewpony Inn, halfway to Kinver, was my favourite green to sit and watch the games. All of us happily walking home to Amblecote and, if it was a moonlit night, we took the canal way back home.'

The Stewpony pub, which I remembered visiting during my time at home, is long gone now, just a memory. It had a fine outdoor swimming pool too.

Bowls in the West Midlands is the "proper" crown green type of bowls, where all of the green can be used, which rises up in the centre, hence the name "crown" and is a much more difficult game to play than the flat green bowls game, in my opinion, and with a biased jack.

I loved playing it and if you sent your bowl incorrectly, even by an inch or two across a crown, you could be miles off the jack or, plenty of times, in the gutter too!

There was also his other love, football, which I believe he must have been quite good at as a lad; "nimble" Mum called him. He was Stourbridge football through and through; his uncle, the trainer at the club, cleaned and studded the players boots ready for the next game, with his wife hoping for a dry match as she had to wash the club's strip after each game, in the tub at home in the back yard.

Billy was in on the action too, being on the committee of the club. Mum said it was a well-known fact that

Billy, on behalf of the Stourbridge club, helped to sell a talented player for £450 to a league team as part of his "scouting" duties for big clubs. Nothing for Grandad, I suspect, except perhaps shillings for a pint. As a comparison, the Amblecote house was bought for £475 in the same era!

But on a Saturday night, after a pint or two, serious Billy became a pub clog dancer of note. Clog dancing being all the rage then. When he got going, he performed a trick of placing his cloth cap on his foot and in an agile movement, flicking it firmly onto his head, apparently never missing!

I would have loved to have seen that because when I knew him, he was already a stern old man. Lived for his "oss racin" (horse racing), on our TV in the communal lounge, scouring the paper before each race for a winner, which I believe he rarely got.

Nearby, there was Netherton, Cradley and Old Hill, noted for its chain-making. 'There were hundreds of tiny homes where, in their gardens, chains were made, in a cottage industry,' said Mum. 'The youngsters hired barrows at two pence a time to take the chains to the works. This was the heart of the Black Country; iron, brick, chain, glassworks and many more trades. Everything could be made in nearby Birmingham and the Black Country, by men of considerable skills. But having a father who was a glassmaker, I knew this industry best,' said Mum. 'Its products were beautiful, but costly to buy; it was worth anyone's time to go and see these works. From the dirty start of molten lead mixture, through to its sulphur-fumed making in the red-hot kilns, and later onto the cutting process. I wondered how anything so delicate could stand the intricate cutting wheels. My own father made wine glasses at Thomas Webb and Sons, in Collis Street, Amblecote, for 43 years.'

Mum saw plenty of the stifling work conditions because, as a child, she had to take her dad's dinner to him at the works, in a basin covered with a red spotted hanky during her lunch break from school, then run back again for the afternoon schooling.

'It was certainly an experience to see red-hot glass being gently blown, by mouth, from a blob at the end of a long tube. Father rolling it with wooden tools to make the foot, leg and actual wine glass. From there, the "takers-in" took it into the kiln,' recalled Mum.

Only small amounts of blown glass is made nowadays; there are cheaper and quicker ways of making glass now. But Grandad worked in the Stourbridge glass industry when it was in its prime, with its grime, heat and deadly fumes issuing through the famous cone-shaped chimneys, which were at the heart of the glass factories, polluting the skies with the ash and fumes from the red-hot kilns. Hence, the glassmaking industry, along with its chain and iron and steel works neighbours, gave the area its Black Country name with miles of towns and countryside shrouded in fumes, fire and smoke. Never has a name been so apt.

At the end, when Grandad had enough and decided to retire, after 43 years of sweat and toil, what did the loyal and dedicated craftsman receive as a retirement present? A glass bowl that's all, worth practically nothing to a glass company, but beautifully engraved with his name. I can't remember any money being handed out to Grandad. Penny-pinching or what, for a stalwart worker, but that's my view.

Grandad's company had a national reputation which was told in a little booklet I have, entitled, *English glass-making, the hand-made process described*, from Thomas Webb's. There is an extract from the *Pottery Gazette* for June 1907 in this booklet, which reads: "Before undergoing her gun-firing trials HMS *Dreadnought* was fitted out exclusively with glass supplied by Thos Webb and Sons Ltd, established 1837. Those trials were exceptionally severe, the concussion being so great as to make the huge vessel heel over, and to drive it sideways several yards through the water. Yet on her return it was found that no glass whatever had been broken during the time she had been at sea, a remarkable testimony to the strength of handmade glass and its power of resisting shock of no ordinary severity."

Pretty good workmanship all round. Testimony to the glassmakers' art and the bravery of its sailors on that ship.

In the following year, 1908, Webb & Sons built an entire glass furnace in an ornate building at the Franco British Exhibition in White City, Shepherd's Bush, London. For 6d, the public could watch glass being made and later cut and decorated and even have a go at glass blowing themselves! Pretty exotic for the turn of the century, I would say.

*The English Glass Making Illustrated Guide* is still in the family, along with a further set of the post cards, both printed and published by Mark & Moody Ltd., Stourbridge, where my mum worked in the bookbinding department for years. The cards illustrate how a handmade wine glass was made. Photo number 1 shows a worker gathering the bowl in the furnace, photo 2; marvering, 3; casting on the stem, 4; chalk-marking the bowl, 5; wetting off, 6; shearing off, 7; opening the bowl, 8; taking in.

Grandad, when he was a frail old man, decided to give Mum's neighbour a wine glass that he'd made many years before, so ruining a set of six, but luckily the neighbour, possibly Mrs Growcot, brought it back to the house and it was put back into the set.

I believe this set of six wine glasses, of no great merit, other than it was handmade in Stourbridge by my grandad, was also the set that, much earlier, Grandad had seen in a second-hand shop in town and, realising he'd made them, bought them. Those glasses I still have.

## CHAPTER TWENTY

# Aunty Kathleen's Story: The Assistant Matron

A unty Kathleen Edwards was my dad's sister, and was born on July 26, 1906. Aunty never married and for most of her life lived alone at the family home – 14 Studley Gate, Wollaston, near Stourbridge – after Dad had left home to get married.

I remember that she was not your average "aunty", all sweets and kind attentions to me. She had a presence, an authority, which she never lost and must have come from her nursing profession.

She rose through the ranks in nursing and finally she was appointed assistant matron, serving at Wordsley Hospital, and in Birmingham. She retired, on grounds of ill health, with that rank, and I am sure, given good health she would have reached matron status.

Dad and his sister Kathleen as young kids photographed on holiday in Rae Pickard's Studio, Queen Street, Rhyl.

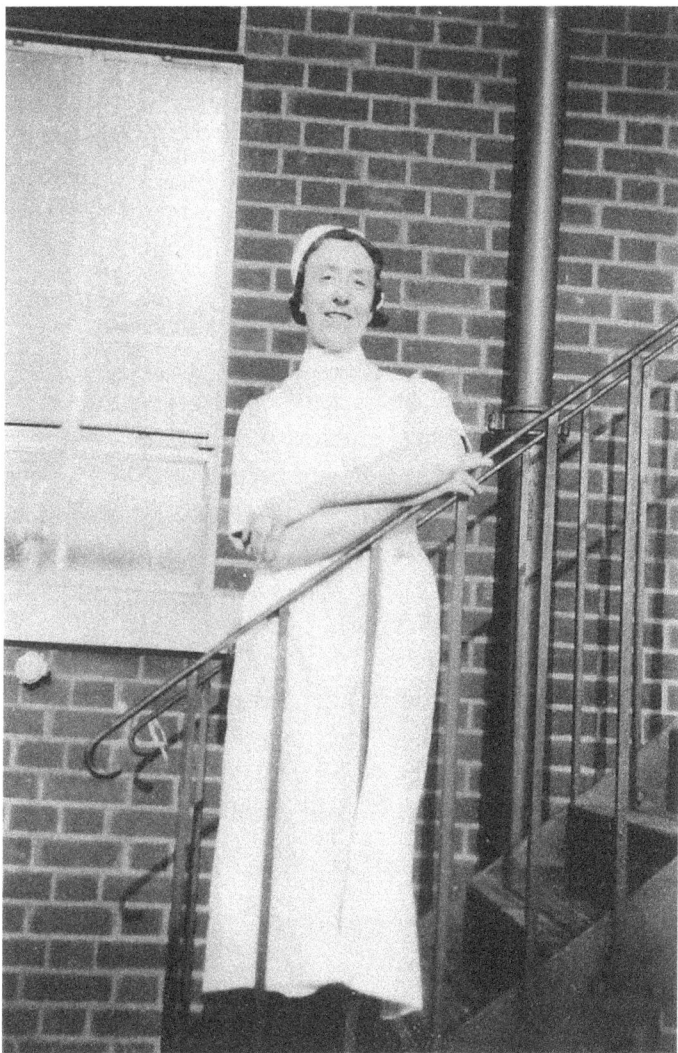

Aunty Kathleen on duty in her nurses' uniform, probably at Birmingham Hospital. She had a lifetime devotion to nursing despite her own serious ill health, rising to assistant matron.

Matrons in those days were like sergeant majors in the army; if they said jump to their staff, they blooming well had to, immediately and without question. Matrons ruled the hospitals then, dare I say it, with an iron fist. It was an exacting job, being responsible for all the wards, patients and all the staff under her in a major accident and emergency hospital in the West Midlands.

Auntie's major problem was ill health all her life. At the start of the twentieth century and before, tuberculosis was a major killer and I think aunty was lucky to survive. Because of a tuberculosis infection her left lung and all her ribs on that side had been removed. She met her major health problems "with fortitude", my brother Dave said.

Dave and I both remember her as an avid lover of puzzles and crosswords. Aunty was an inveterate purchaser of household gadgets; you know, the sort of items sold through catalogues in the *Radio Times*, that sort of thing. The funny thing is, though, she hardly ever used them. I used to find them in drawers, small flashlights, etc., all unused.

As a toddler, I have memories of the house too. She had a piano, but I was fascinated by the piano stool in front of it. You could screw it up and down to get the required height and I remember it kept me quiet for hours.

I remember the garden very well, smaller than ours at 41 Vicarage Road, very well because there was nowhere to play. It was not made for a small child to romp about in, having glorious flower beds everywhere and a tiny lawn just large enough for a couple of chairs. She loved her garden and I remember her green gardening gloves hung on a hook in the kitchen.

Dave, the eldest, has other, earlier memories of the house in Studley Gate. He said it was the last of several houses the family had. 'I suppose I was about six when Grandad Edwards died. I was standing by the front door and I could hear Mum, Dad and Aunty Kathleen discussing whether I should see the body which was in one of the upstairs bedrooms. I did, for which I am grateful. I cannot remember much at all of Nanna. She must have passed away previously,' Dave said.

I have Christmas memories of Aunty, when she was part of the celebrations at home. She was a tiny woman, very frail. She always ate like a bird; I suppose she had to watch what she ate due to her health. She was very particular with what she ate. I have always remembered one phrase she used at meal times. Pushing away her plate or dish, she would politely say, 'I've had an elegant sufficiency, thank you.' Funny, how some memories of over 60 years ago just stick with you.

In later years, she had her friend, Ruth Jones, as a companion; they got on really well as she was in nursing too. After Aunty died, we had to clear the house of her belongings. I was in her bedroom, looking in the bottom of a wardrobe, when I found a head! It was a dummy's head with a wig on it! Phew. My heart missed a beat. Aunty had always had very fine, thinning hair, but I never saw her wear a wig. Another item she bought, but never used!

I still have a nursing medal, which was bestowed on her, in its own posh box. It is inscribed "1938", so ten years before the introduction of the NHS, from Hallam Hospital, West Bromwich, Birmingham. That hospital started out as part of a work house, and in 1925 became an isolation hospital, for the horrible tuberculosis disease, one suspects. The medal is a bronze colour, not gold, and has no assay marks on it. Long service to Hallam Hospital, I reckon.

She died of a heart attack on July 3, 1985, aged 79, in Wordsley Hospital. I feel sad that it was only ill health which prevented her from becoming a full matron, I'm sure. She deserved that for her dedication to the service of looking after people in her wonderful chosen profession, despite her own physical frailties, with a sharp mind and an empathy for looking after her patients and staff.

## CHAPTER TWENTY-ONE

# Military Men in the Family

W e have naval, army and air force wartime connections in the family including Dad, who helped make steel for the war effort in a vulnerable Wolverhampton factory and was a member of the ARP (Air Raid Precautions) at night.

The naval connection is not exactly a family connection, for "Uncle" Peter was not a family member, but he was my godfather.

My earliest recollection of Uncle Peter was occasionally having to walk to The Fish, Amblecote, where Peter was waiting in his car to take Dad, a non-car owner at the time, to work in Wolverhampton and sometimes tell him that Dad wasn't well, with a cold for flu or suchlike and would not be coming to work that day. Neither of our families, you see, had phones. We'd smile and Peter would continue to work. I would have to double back from The Fish into Stourbridge to make the first lesson at school.

Dad's cousin Gordon Homer in the pioneering First World War Royal Flying Corps, the forerunner of the Royal Air Force (RAF). The RFC flash can be seen on Gordon's left shoulder.

Peter worked alongside Dad at Bayliss Jones and Bayliss in Wolverhampton, but during the Second World War, he was in the Royal Navy. He encountered a fate worse than death, it could be said, as he was on board battle cruiser HMS *Repulse*, together with the *Prince of Wales,* which were sent to Singapore on practically a suicide mission by Prime Minister Winston Churchill; critically without destroyer escort, my brother said. Both mighty ships were sunk by the Japanese with bombs and submarines. Over 1500 men were killed while Peter, a non-swimmer, was forced to jump overboard as his ship quickly sank. Clinging onto wreckage, he was rescued by the Japanese.

Peter spent two years in Changi prisoner of war camp, was eventually repatriated, but he was a broken man; he was never the same Peter again. He returned to work, but I remember him as a very timid, nervous man, who was a loner, never marrying and living alone after his mother died. He never spoke to anyone in the family of his obviously traumatic time spent as a prisoner of war, as far as I know. God only knows what he witnessed; he did go regularly to a club in London, in Pall Mall, I recall, for war veterans and got comradeship but not closure among fellow servicemen, who similar war stories of their own to share.

Uncle Peter did, on occasion, make visits to the family home, and at one time I had a Japanese car, but this had to be kept a secret from him.

As I began to write the family history, I was shocked to learn from brother Dave that once, while driving my dad to work, Peter accused him of being a spy, such was the fragility of his mental health. No counselling in those days, just had to get on with it. "Pull yourself together, man" was the advice then. So sad. Nonetheless, he was a hero.

Back to the First World War, and a story involving the formation of the Royal Flying Corps (RFC), the forerunner of the Royal Air Force. It concerns Gordon Homer, a cousin of my dad's.

The RFC started life as part of the British Army before and during the First World War. With aircraft in very early stages of development, they were first utilised by the army for photographic reconnaissance and helping pinpoint areas for the artillery. Only later were planes used for battles in the air with German and British aces, strafing missions and lobbing bombs out of the cockpit at targets on the ground. Alarmingly, for the occupants, parachutes were not available to any pilots during WWI.

Excitedly, when told of this story, I thought, *wow, an RFC First World War flying ace in the family!* But no, Gordon was an engine fitter for the brave pilots, flying off into the unknown skies in their "stringbag" biplanes, like the Sopwich Camel which he must have worked on.

We have information from the British Royal Airforce Airmen's Service Records 1912-1939. Gordon first enlisted in the army, February 10, 1917, aged 18. He transferred to the Royal Flying Corps and was a founder member of the RAF, when it came into being on 1 April

1918, joining 125 Squadron as a fitter and turner. His service number was 60590 and he was stationed at Thetford, Norfolk and Martlesham Heath, amongst other places.

The document states he was 5-foot, 5-and-a-half inches tall, with chest measurement of 33 inches. Not a big chap! Gordon transferred to the RAF Reserve, December 14, 1919. What we don't know is whether Gordon saw any action in France.

A lovely advertisement for the Royal Flying Corps (military wing) said "vacancies exist" for men aged 18 to 30, with pay from 2 shillings per day for air mechanics to warrant officers at 9 shillings a day. They were to apply to the RFC via South Farnborough, Hants. Men selected to be trained as "flyers" were to receive a further two to four shillings per day plus "free clothing, and necessaries, quarters, rations, fuel and light and medical attendance". The last item was probably vital!

Gordon married Vera Johnson in 1925 in Kidderminster, only a few miles from Stourbridge. At 40, Gordon was working in the carpet trade, for which Kidderminster is famous, maintaining looms. His birth date was given as January 15, 1899. He died in January, 1985 in Kidderminster, aged 86.

Also in the First World War, we had Captain John Henry Skidmore of the Grenadier Guards. He was from my mother's side of the family and was the eldest legitimate son of Mum's gran, Liz Skidmore; 'A well-built, comely lass,' said Mum.

However, there is an odd thing about the captain. His name was John Henry George, born to Mr Henry George (George being his dad's surname), who Liz married. But when he enlisted into the army, in 1890, it was under the name of Skidmore, his mother's name. Why, we have no idea. It gets more confused, as Liz was left at the altar, pregnant. She gave birth to a son and family folklore had this to be John Henry, later captain. Only it wasn't. We know through research the name of the illegitimate child was Cornelius. He was brought up with two other children from Liz and her husband, Mr George.

Mr George was killed when horses he used for work at Palfrey's Skin Works, Stourbridge, bolted after a high wind near Wollaston Church blew paper into the face of one of them, and the reins, which Mr George had told his firm needed changing, broke.

Liz later married Mr Henry Jones and they had a further four children; Sarah, Clara, Joe and my mum's mum, Nellie, the youngest.

In the 1881 census, John Henry was living at 70 Bowling Green Road, Stourbridge, with Henry and Liz Jones. Ten years later, in the 1891 census, JH is shown as a single male, 19, with his occupation listed as "private" and his address St Martin in the Fields, Strand, London, at the St Georges Barracks, Trafalgar Square. In 1901 he cannot be found in the census as he was serving abroad.

In 1911, he is a married man and a lieutenant, 38 years old, living in Marlborough Lines, Aldershot,

Farnborough, Hampshire. Aldershot being a military town and he was at Malplaquet Barracks.

But before that, Mum wrote in her book: "Nell (her mum) absolutely adored her military brother. She was so proud at 14 years old, seeing him off on the Stourbridge train in all his posh army gear".

She once visited London to visit him and his wife. Mum continued: "The captain got her to go and buy some lozenges for his throat and little auburn-haired Nell was on the barracks parade square when the old devil got his men to surround her to embarrass her!"

After he died Captain Jack's pension eventually went to Liz; it was never known what happened to Jack's wife. Nell (mum's mum) filled in the forms every month for Gran, who could read, but not write. The pension kept Gran in comfort in her very old age. Nell was given a silver thimble for filling in all these forms over many years, which is still in the family.

His gravestone in Stourbridge cemetery says "Captain John Henry Skidmore, 1914-18, died 8 November, 1918". The other information is that he was in the 314th Prisoner of War Company Labour Corps, British Army, with rank of Honorary Lieutenant and Quarter Master, Captain, Regiment Grenadier Guards and Labour Corps. I believe he could have been wounded and transferred out of the Guards to the Labour Corps.

I also believe he died at home, in Stourbridge, of the infamous outbreak of Spanish flu, which killed millions of civilians and soldiers around the end of the war.

## CHAPTER TWENTY-TWO

# Harold, *BlackCountryman* Editor

One of the friends and colleagues who "popped in" over many, many years to see my parents at 41 Vicarage Road, Amblecote, was Harold Parsons, *Blackcountryman* magazine editor, and gag (joke) writer to some of the star comedians of the day, firstly on radio then TV.

Mum and Dad must have gone to see them in their house sometimes, but I cannot recall it. But Harold always had a car and Dad didn't drive or own a car until he was 50, so it was probably easier for Harold and Joan to come to Amblecote.

Dad had met and befriended Harold when they both worked for many years at Bayliss Jones and Bayliss steel works. And Harold, I remember, was a regular visitor, first from his Dudley home with his wife, and later when they moved to Kinver, known as the Switzerland of the Midlands, Harold said.

I remember Harold who unfortunately was never of robust health with chest and breathing problems.

He had a slight speech impediment, which never held him back in his life as a professional writer. His upbringing in the coal and the grime of coal fires and open range cooking as a boy, he knew in hindsight, had done nothing to help his poorly chest.

I believe Harold was a bit of an inspiration to me, proving that you could become a writer and make a living.

I found out my copy of his autobiography, *Substance and Shadow, a Black Country Writer*, to reread as I started to write this book. It is a short book, published in 1982, and stuck to Harold's principles of not overwriting anything. But it is a little gem and brings to life his early childhood in Dudley, his struggles and the tough living conditions which were prevalent in those far off days in the Black Country.

Harold was born in 1919 at Woodside, Dudley. His family had a small shop, which was situated in the front room of the house in Salop Street, Dudley, where they moved to in 1923 and where Harold lived for 25 years. The shop served cheap toys and hardware to the local community. Toys sold well for Christmas and hardware for the rest of the year.

The introduction of libraries, where you could actually go round and choose your own books, came in 1933, and were a godsend to Harold. Before that, lenders had to ask for the book they wanted at Dudley Library and it was brought to them, as they waited.

It was in 1934 that Harold got a job at Bayliss Jones and Bayliss and where, later, he met my father and a lifetime friendship began.

Much later, Harold achieved fame as a gag writer for radio comedian, Charlie Chester, MBE, who later transferred to TV. He was a star from the 1940s right up to the 1990s and like lots of comedians, he paid gag writers for jokes. The pair had a good partnership for many years and Chester had great respect for the abilities of Harold to come up with the right kind of material for his act. I do remember watching Charlie Chester on the Esther Rantzen TV Show, possibly *That's Life*, reading his "odes" to camera wearing a dinner jacket and tie.

It was the advent of radio which made many stars in the 40s after the introduction of electricity to people's houses in earlier years, for simple lighting and heating at first, before groundbreaking technology brought nationwide broadcasting from the BBC.

Radio was, if you like, the Facebook and internet of its day. It brought music, laughter through many top comedy shows, and up-to-date news broadcasts. Quite simply, it was a revolution. Changed our lives forever.

Charlie Chester had a radio show in the late 40s called *Stand Easy*, which drew in 10-12 million listeners each week! That's how big radio was. As a comparison, the first episode of TV soap opera *EastEnders* drew in 13 million viewers, apparently.

Harold also did joke writing for many other star names, remembered more than Charlie Chester, such as Benny Hill, Tommy Cooper, and Morecombe and Wise before some of them had made the big time. All this time, Harold still worked for BJB with my dad and never made the decision to go full-time in the precarious show business profession. But for a time, Harold was making as much, if not more, money at gag writing than he was working for the company!

As most things do, over time, work changes, sometimes fizzles out, and you are not so much in demand. He was not downhearted and continued writing all his life, being paid, making a bit of money.

Harold did make it to 25 years' service at BJB for which he received £10. Being a writer, he immediately wrote an acerbic piece on the company's long service awards ceremony, which the *Manchester Guardian* printed and paid him 12 guineas! It was more than the company paid him for 25 years of service. The "pay out" was equivalent of two pence a week!

In his autobiography, he says the *Guardian* printed "Gross of Servants", and was one of his finest pieces, which was republished many times.

Harold took to writing for magazines about plumbing and heating, caravans and caravan holidays, children's strip cartoons; he turned his hand to anything, as a fine all-round writer. This eventually led him, when he was a full-time freelance, to start editing *The Blackcountryman* magazine, among many things, which he did for over 15 years for the Black Country Society, supervising no less than 83 editions. He came up with many dozens of book ideas as his interest in the Black Country history increased.

The Society's first book, in 1968, which he helped produce, was called *Black Country Stories*, which sold over 30,000 copies; an amazing publishing success story.

The Black Country Society has gone on to even greater things, promoting interest in the past, present and future and still publishes *The Blackcountryman* magazine quarterly to its many members worldwide, with features and articles about the Black Country, organises talks, and the publication of books.

I do wish I had kept some of the old *Blackcountryman* magazines, edited by Harold and so beloved by Mum and Dad, but they have gone. My brother, Dave, told me he still has one prized edition of *The Blackcountryman*, of spring, 1989, volume 2, in his Hobart, Tasmania, home.

Harold wrote two unpublished novels from his early days, but did publish *Warwickshire – History, People and Places* (1975) and *A Thousand Events in the 19c Black Country* (1982).

This is just some of Harold's work. He was a stalwart and continued to write through his poor health. I have used bits of information from Harold's own autobiography, *Substance and Shadow*, published by

Barbryn Press Ltd., 61 Cornwall St, Birmingham B3 2EB, printed by Reliance Printing Works, Halesowen, West Midlands. I expect it is long out of print, but I hope giving out these details may help people get hold of a copy, and I won't get into trouble over copyright, which Harold owned.

# CHAPTER TWENTY-THREE

# Family Puddlers and Nailers!

What have blacksmiths, colliers, labourers, puddlers, brickmakers, waterman, glassmakers, farmers and nailers have in common?

They were all jobs which just some of my ancestors had, going back to the 18$^{th}$ century!

Yes, diligent work, not my own, I must add, has discovered names of family ancestors, going way back!

Going back to great x5 grandparents on my dad's side, we have the names of Francis Roper, who married Margaret Cookson in Broseley, in 1727. In the list of great x4 grandparents we have Daniel Fownes or Fones, married to Mary Oakley of Sedgley in 1776, he a collier.

The great x3 grandparents gives us a brickmaker, plus James Wassall and Sarah Pearson getting married in 1817, and James of Kingswinford, a waterman. Someone who made his living on the local "cut".

I have always adored narrowboats, and their steady 4mph *chuff chuff* gait, and me walking the towpaths, probably in the very footsteps of my forebear! Possibly he would have used horses in his daily life, if he transported goods on the canals of the Black Country, during their first golden age, before the railways cut into their business.

We have Charles Gritton, married to Elizabeth; Charles was born in 1784 in Kingswinford and probably died in 1854. His profession was that of a glassmaker. We had my grandfather, Billy Hicks, who lived with us at 41 Vicarage Road, Amblecote and was a glassmaker with Webbs of Amblecote for nigh on 50 years, but he was not, we know now, the first glassmaker in the family! This leads me to all sorts of questions; which glass factory did Charles work in, for how long, for he is also down on the census as a greengrocer. Discoveries have since unearthed even more glassmaking people in the family on Grandad's side too.

There are two interesting occupations which have come up in research; we have two family members who were nailers and one puddler in an iron works. Our nailers were great x3 grandparents, one a woman and one a man. Mary Mason, who became the wife of Henry Fownes, was born in Coseley 1789, and just a name for the other nailer; John Homer. Nailers were pretty much at the bottom of the "food chain" as far as jobs went in those dusty, grime and coal days. It was a cottage industry involving not only men, as we see with our name of Mary Mason, but children too.

Mainly Black Country nailers were to be found in small workshops or their own dwellings in yards. It was an arduous and hard life, often paid by the factory bosses with tokens to spend in particular shops, not real money. They were tied to that factory, who they supplied handmade nails too. A lot would have been used as horse nails, when the horse was king, as well as industrial uses, I expect.

A top nailer could make 24,000 nails a week and the industry at one time numbered 50,000 nailers around Sedgley, Gornal, Lye, Halesowen, Old Hill, Dudley and other towns. The cottage industry died out when nails could be machine-made as machines took over their jobs.

We turn to our puddler ancestor; Thomas Homer, born in 1812 in Kingswinford. A puddler worked in an ironworks and the definition is of a workman who turns pig iron into wrought iron by puddling. Henry Cort had the patent for his puddling furnace in 1784. Molten pig iron was stirred (hence puddling) in a furnace, which made wrought iron, which had many useful industrial applications.

So that's what our ancestor, Thomas Homer, was involved in. Pretty much a hot and sweaty atmosphere to work in (which I can verify having stood next to the giant furnaces at Round Oak Steel Works, Brierley Hill, in the late 1960s). The same sweatbox environment as our glassmaker ancestor, Charles Gritton, and others had as a daily grind, plus our many blacksmiths; my dad's father, Richard Edwards (1871-1949) included, in Pensnett, and another Thomas Homer (1843-1907) born in Kingswinford.

Part of our family from the Hicks side came from Shropshire. Research has led to many Hicks names in the tiny Shropshire village of Ditton Priors, nestling under the Brown Clee. Richard Hicks (1769-1836) is buried there, as is his wife Elizabeth Littleford (1778-1851) and some of their children. A hunt in the churchyard found no gravestone with any of the names we were looking for, unfortunately. For the remote hill families, life must have been tough, easily cut off in hard winters by snowdrifts, with work increasingly difficult to find to sustain life.

I presume the Hicks' had to relocate to the Black Country as agricultural work in the countryside dried up and many thousands upon thousands of people were forced to move from rural villages and locations to find jobs in burgeoning towns, as the industrial revolution rewrote the historical landscape of the country forever.

We discovered, through Tricia, our genealogist friend, possibly a unique entry on a census document. In the 1851 census our ancestor, William Cox (50), of Back Lane, Kingswinford put down he was a farmer, out of business, alongside his wife, Mary Ann Cox (57), born in Shropshire. But sensationally, their children, Mary Ann (20), put down under occupation "anything you please", which was crossed out. Her brother, William's (17) occupation entry was also crossed out, but the younger children, Henrietta (15), also had inscribed, "anything you please", as did Emelia (12). So, the dad was an unemployed farmer and his children were desperately asking for any work at all. Hard times for the family indeed. Tricia, in 39 years of genealogy had never seen such an entry in all her researches.

The heartfelt entries came 130 years before that great writer Alan Bleasdale wrote his own immortal phrase for Yosser Hughes; "Gizza job" (give us a job) about unemployed Liverpudlians in the BBC's *Boys from the Blackstuff* serial, during the Thatcher era. Different times, different reasons, but the census entry of 1851 is the eloquent equal in despair. Desperate people who plead to be given a job, in the hardest of hard times, even to the extent of writing it in the occupation column in the national census, a sentiment similar to that of Yosser's plea, "Gizza job".

The strangest name to be uncovered in our family is that of my 4x great aunt, baptised in Holy Trinity Church, Wordsley, on July 3, 1836 as Azubah Doolittle Simpson! Some name for a little girl. Azubah, in the Bible, was the mother of Jehoshaphat. And in Hebrew, Azubah means desolation. Well, a 4x aunt called Azubah Doolittle Simpson, later Cartwright; that's different,' said Tricia. We have yet to discover why she was also Doolittle!

## CHAPTER TWENTY-FOUR

# The Oldest Family Book

One book, in the possession of the family, is 353 years old!

It's called *Systema Agriculturae, or, The Mystery of Husbandry Discovered*, written by John Worlidge, who often called himself J W Gent, published 1669. Yes, that's right, 1669, no misprint here. It is leather-bound, with faults, but in what I would call a fairish condition for its over 350 years of age, and is a first edition, a fact verified to me by Bonhams of New Bond Street, London, in 2005. There are indeed many editions of this book.

I was particularly inspired by the 1669 date when I was researching it as it was only three years after the Great Fire of London, and was published in Fleet Street. More exactly, "Printed by T Johnson for Samuel Speed, near the Inner Temple Gate in Fleet Street, 1669".

The book department of Bonhams, the leading auctioneers, were quick to point out that it was "not particularly unusual in this respect, as printers were very quick to get back to work after the Fire, producing pamphlets and books just as before".

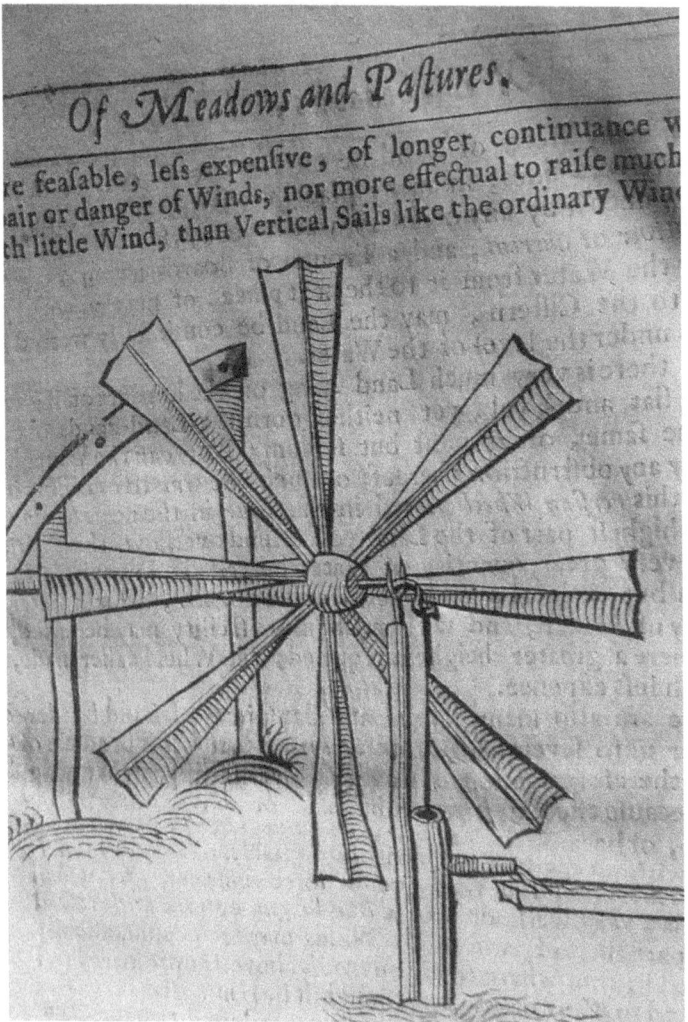

An illustration from the family book on agriculture, printed in Fleet Street, London in 1669, showing an early wind pump for raising water.

This was a little disappointing to me.

Worlidge was an early expert on agriculture to put pen to paper for the good of his fellow man. Some of his works were revolutionary and he distilled many ideas of others in the past too, which were carried out by most farmers in the land and were of much merit. Wikipedia notes him as one of the first British agriculturists to discuss the importance of farming as an industry.

Our book is annotated on many of his illustrated pages with handwriting, so was used as a working book by a farmer or one working in agriculture somewhere, but whom, we know not. It would be thrilling to know whose hand made these plentiful notes in our book, and it would be nice if they were ancestors of the family.

Inside the front cover there are two names; Hugh and Jasper Willmott of Wolverley, Worcestershire and I did speak to someone in, I believe, Wolverley, but no intelligible information was forthcoming.

In handwritten form on another, partly distressed page are the words "May 6" (year date gone, I'm afraid), but underneath, "Upper Mitton, Parish of Hartlebury, and county of Worcestershire". At one stage, it was a Worcestershire book, maybe even from when it was printed.

Was one of our ancestors a farmer in that area? We don't know.

Written in "Shakespearean" English, with "f" for "s", part of an extensive preface is as follows: "This Country life improves and exercises the most noble and excellent parts of our Intellects, and affords the best opportunities to the insatiable humane Spirit, to Contemplate and Meditate on, and to penetrate into, and discover the obscure, and hitherto occult Mysteries and secrets of Nature; The fixity, or mobility of the Earth, the nature of the Air, it weight and divers mutations, the flux and reflux of the Sea, the nature and matter of the Comets, Meteors etc., the Mystery of Vegetation, the nature of Animals and their different Species, the discovery and improvement of Minerals, and to attain the highest perfections in Science and Art, yea this condition capacitates a man to the full to the study and practice of the most Secret and Mystical things Nature affords, if adapted thereunto."

It is a very learned tome and wonderful to read. Before Worlidge gets his teeth into all the various aspects of agriculture, he has a "Catalogue of such authors who have written of agriculture or of some branch thereof, and were consulted with in the composure of the subsequent treatise."

He gives credit to those who had gone before him, to Greek authors, including Pliny the Elder (I never thought I would ever get to write that name; the legendary Pliny!) who wrote the world's first encyclopaedia. His *Natural History*, alluded to by Worlidge, had more than a million words in 37 volumes. He mentions "Butler" who wrote a history of bees and says it's an incomparable piece. With a planet seemingly intent of wiping out the crucial bees, I find this revelation of the great worth of bees in the

17$^{th}$ century mind-bogglingly intuitive. There are many other authors he gives credit to, plus books like the *Consideration concerning Common Fields and Enclosure*, Sir Hugh Plat for his *Jewel House of Art and Nature, A treatise of Silk-worms,* published by Mr Hartlib and *The Country-mans Recreation, Or the Art of Planting, Grafting, and Gardening, in Three Books.* Many more great names in the history of agriculture are also listed.

When I contacted the British Library, Early Printed Collections Department, in London regarding the book, they confirmed there were 28 locations of copies of this work around the world, including, among others, The National Library of Wales, Birmingham University Library, Cambridge University Library, Cambridge University, Trinity College, National Library of Scotland, Edinburgh University Library, National History Museum, Senate House Library, University of London, Oxford University, Bodleian Library, University of British Columbia, Vancouver, Francis Bacon Foundation, Inc. Claremont, California, University of California, Los Angeles, William Andrews Clark Memorial, California, University of Chicago, Illinois, Harvard University, Cambridge, Massachusetts, University of Texas, Austin, Texas and the University of Tokyo, Japan.

Fantastic! I was very impressed. More news came towards the end of the British Library letter to me: "Sets in bad condition are usually of little or no value". It seems even books of that age must be perfect to have monetary value, although, of course, as a historical object and one for intensive study, both from an agricultural point of view, and culturally, it is invaluable. There's enough information in the book, a schoolteacher friend of mine once said, for someone to get a couple of university degrees!

So that's is, that's where I let it lie; I tried to track down who the book might have been used by, through information on the inner cover, but found no joy.

I am led to believe, a 350-year-old book, with not many first editions remaining, is of little or no value, monetary-wise; a few hundred pound was quoted. But, as a treasure trove of the history of agriculture in all its aspects, invaluable.

There is the family mystery; just how and why our family ended up in possession of this fascinating old book is not known. Perhaps someone reading this book might just give us a clue!

www.ingramcontent.com/pod-product-compliance
Lightning Source LLC
Chambersburg PA
CBHW051827040426
42447CB00006B/411